CLOZE THE GAP!

Exercises in Integrating and Developing Language Skills

REVISED EDITION

BY VALERIE WHITESON

ALTA BOOK CENTER PUBLISHERS

Senior Editor:	Aarón Berman, Alta Book Center
Book Design:	Andrea Reider, San Francisco, USA
Cover Design and Production:	Cleve Gallat, San Francisco, USA

ALTA BOOK CENTER PUBLISHERS—SAN FRANCISCO

14 Adrian Court
Burlingame, California 94010 USA
Phone: 800 ALTA/ESL • 650.692.1285
Fax: 800 ALTA/FAX • 650.692.4654
Email: ALTAESL@AOL.COM
Website: WWW.ALTAESL.COM

ISBN 1-882483-25-1

Contents

Credits

Photo and Illustration Credits:

Page 8   Photos by Ilka Hartmann, San Francisco USA

Page 16   Photo © Warner Bros. Inc.

Page 40   Photo by Ilka Hartmann, San Francisco USA

Page 82   Photo by Daniel Cowan, Port of Miami

Page 88   Photo by Ilka Hartmann, San Francisco USA

Page 102   Photo by Ilka Hartmann, San Francisco USA

Page 112   Photo by Ilka Hartmann, San Francisco USA

Page 132   Photo © The Walt Disney Company

Page 152   Illustration Courtesy of University Publishing Projects

Page 162   Photo © CBS Inc.

Story Credits:

What's in a Name, © Scholastic U.S. Express. Used by permission of Scholastic, Inc.

Coming to America, © Scholastic U.S. Express. Used by permission of Scholastic, Inc.

I's No Act, © Scholastic U.S. Express. Used by permission of Scholastic, Inc.

The American Dream, © Scholastic U.S. Express. Used by permission of Scholastic, Inc.

Mary Nguyen, © Scholastic U.S. Express. Used by permission of Scholastic, Inc.

The Books That Changed My Life, © Scholastic Voice. Used by permission of Scholastic, Inc.

Jokes, © Scholastic Scope. Used by permission of Scholastic, Inc.

Disneyland, © Scholastic Literary Calvacade. Used by permission of Scholastic, Inc.

Every effort has been made to trace and acknowledge ownership of copyright. The publishers will be glad to make suitable arrangements with any copyright holder whom it has not been possible to contact.

Introduction

To the teacher:

The aim of *Cloze The Gap* is to develop and integrate the skills of intermediate learners of English as a second or foreign language.

This workbook contains twenty passages in which words have been deleted (rational cloze procedure). The deleted words are grammatical and lexical items which often cause difficulties for non-native speakers of English. The student has to decide which words best fill the gaps and write them in to complete the passage.

The passages have been chosen from a wide range of newspaper and magazine articles, stories, advertisements, brochures, and letters which were originally published in different parts of the English-speaking world. For the most part they are reproduced in their original form. They were chosen because of their interest to young adults and are graded according to difficulty. Students will be introduced to many different styles and registers and will, hopefully, become sensitive to different kinds of English.

Prereading questions and dictionary work help to prepare the students to fill the gaps in the cloze passages. Each of the words in the dictionary exercise has been glossed according to A. S. Hornby's *Oxford Student's Dictionary of American English* (1983). The phonetic transcription of the words is given both in American and British pronunciations. The American pronunciation comes from the same text; whereas, the British transcription comes from A. S. Hornby's *Oxford Advanced Learner's Dictionary of Current English* (1983) – both published by Oxford University Press. The key to the phonetic symbols can be found in the Appendix.

Follow up vocabulary exercises are included to recycle and spiral useful words which will help students to increase their word power. The language exercise in each unit helps students to focus on grammar, style, and register problems which might cause difficulty. Comprehension questions allow the teacher to check if the students have understood the main ideas of the passage. The answers to these comprehension questions form the basis of a composition exercise which enables the student to write a paragraph which is a summary of the passage.

Follow up discussion and composition topics are suggested to encourage students to transfer some of the vocabulary and ideas in the cloze passages to their own written or spoken English.

Valerie Whiteson
Evergreen Valley College
San Jose, California USA

To the student:

The aim of *Cloze The Gap* is to develop and integrate the skills of intermediate learners of English as a second or foreign language.

This workbook contains twenty passages in which words have been deleted. The deleted words are grammatical and lexical items which often cause difficulties for non-native speakers of English. You have to decide which words best fill the gaps and write them in their appropriate form to complete the passage.

The passages have been chosen from newspaper and magazine articles, stories, advertisements, brochures and letters which were originally published in different parts of the English speaking world. They were chosen because of their interest to young adults from fifteen-years-old and up. You will be introduced to many different kinds of English and will, hopefully, become sensitive to them.

Instructions for Completing a Cloze Passage

Before you begin to fill in the blank spaces with a suitable word, scan the whole passage in order to get an idea of the subject matter and other important information, such as whether the passage is about many people or one person; a boy/man or a girl/woman; is it written in the past, present, or future? It's a good idea to fill in the easy words first.

When you fill in the words, check the following:

1. *part of speech*
   Do you need a noun, verb, adjective, article, adverb, pronoun, or preposition?

2. *tense*
   Look for words to help you such as **before, after, while,** or **now.**

3. *fixed expressions*
   Phrasal verbs, such as look (for)
   Idioms, such as cried her (heart) out

4. *context*
   Has the word been mentioned before? Is the word you need closely connected to another word in the text?

5. *singular/plural*
   Verbs, pronouns, and articles must match the relevant items in the text, such as:
   "His advice is good."
   "The water in the river flows rapidly."
   "They asked us for some information."
   "The teacher asked the children who their teacher was."

6. *capital letters*

    If the blank comes immediately after a period, then the word you fill in must begin with a capital letter.

7. *spelling*

    Try to avoid confusing words which sound the same or similar, but are spelled differently, such as **where/were; too/to/two; their/there.**

8. *using clues*

    (i) Punctuation can help you. Certain connectors like ***however,*** and ***therefore,*** come before a comma at the beginning of a sentence and between two commas in the middle of the sentence. For example, "That information, ***however,*** was of no use to her."

    (ii) Words like ***and*** and ***but*** can also be helpful. After the first word you need a similar word or structure. For example, "I like listening to music and reading books." After the second word, you need a contrast, such as "She enjoys driving a car but hates riding a bicycle."

Tri Nguyen **Ken Tali** *José Rosemberg Tennen*

Mary Lou Cabral *Taxi Khek* Juana Menchú

Harvey Redak **Clara Orellana Almendares**

Kim-Ngan Golden Oscar Cisneros **Louisa Rogers**

Suzuki Yamada **Liu Jenhon** *Xochitl Temotzin*

Mary Arnold *Preteep Kiatitanakorn* **Susan Silverman**

Yoshi Nakamura Dick Robbins **Ahmed El-Krim**

David Comanchero Paolo Cecceti *Morteza Radi*

Kenichi Tanaka *Elsa Yuriko* **Vladimir Belyak**

Jean Pierre Eudier Guadalupe Cuauhtémoc Moctezuma

Penelope Papas **Anton Zajac** *Iago Fidani*

Mary Sullivan *Flora Achebe* **Bruce Stone**

Svetlana Senavskaya **Giulia Fiorini** *Ingrid Anderson*

Ilka Klimek *Maureen O'Brien* **Kenji Yamamoto**

Rembrant Ramijn Conrad Kraus **Gabriel D'Annunzio**

Pablo Javier Ronquillo **Leonid Sheykman**

Huayna Atahualpa Boghos Tajian *Peter Linato*

Parveen Singh Cleveland Gallaso **Galina Buyko**

Eina Guinto Magelin Tolentino Rea Franjetic

Moses Mandela Robert Ward Reeder **Jane Wong**

Names from Around the World

1

What's in a Name?

Before you begin trying to find a good word to fill in the gaps in the cloze passage, think about the following questions: How did you get your name? Is there a difference between the way people in other countries decide on a name for their children? What are the names of your pets? Who named them? If you have children one day, what will you name them? Why? Do you like the idea of nicknames? Why? Do they exist in other countries? You might like to discuss these questions with your teacher and the whole class or with one or two classmates. You could also write the answer to these questions in a journal.

Dictionary Exercise

The passage, **What's in a Name,** is about names. Some of the words in the passage may be difficult for you because they have more than one meaning. Read through a list of these words with their dictionary definitions. Try to predict which definition is most correct for a passage about names.

a. **ancestor** [NOUN] /'æn,sestə(r)/
   i.   a person from whom one is descended; forbear
   ii. an early kind; forerunner

b. **ceremony** [NOUN] *North American* /'serə,mouni/ *British* /'serɪmənɪ/
   i.   a set of formal acts proper to a special occasion, as a religious rite
   ii. behavior that follows rigid etiquette
   iii. a) formality
        b) empty formality

c. **culture** [NOUN] *North American* /ˈkəltʃər/ *British* /ˈkʌltʃə(r)/
   i.   cultivation of the soil
   ii. a growth of bacteria in a prepared substance
   iii. improvement of the mind and/or manners
   iv. development by special training or care
   v.   the skills and arts of a given people in a given period or civilization

d. **delicate** [ADJECTIVE] /'delɪkɪt/
   i.   pleasing in its lightness and/or mildness
   ii. beautifully fine in its texture and/or workmanship
   iii. slight and subtle
   iv. easily damaged
   v.   frail in health
   vi. a) needing careful handling
        b) showing tact and consideration
   vii. finely sensitive

e. to **pick** [VERB] /pɪk/
   i.   to pierce or dig up with something pointed
   ii. to probe or scratch so as to remove or clear something from
   iii. to gather (flowers, berries, etc.)
   iv. to choose, select
   v.   to provoke (a quarrel or fight)

f. to **stretch** [VERB] /stretʃ/
   i.   to reach out; extend
   ii. to draw out to full extent or to greater size
   iii. to cause to extend too far; strain
   iv. to strain in interpretation; scope

After you have completed the cloze passage, go back to these words. Did you predict the correct definition of the word? You might like to compare your choice with other students in your class. If you don't agree, check your answer with your teacher. You will have another exercise in this unit in which you will be asked to use these words.

What's in a Name?

In most cultures, children are named by their parents. In the U.S., most parents choose a name for their child before it is born. But in some places, babies are not named right away. In parts of Africa, parents wait until children survive their early years. Then parents may name their 1_____ Joy or Luck to show 2_____ happiness. In Laos, a Hmong boy gets his first name when he's three days 3_____. When he grows up, a ceremony is held to give 4_____ a new name. The ceremony takes place after he 5_____ his own child.

Cambodians say that a 6_____ name lives forever, so parents are careful to choose 7_____ with good meanings for their children. A Cambodian girl may 8_____ named for a delicate flower. A Cambodian boy's name may suggest strength or honesty. In Vietnam, 9_____, a person's name may mean something good or 10_____.

Children in the U.S. are often named for relatives. 11_____ some parents pick a name just because they like 12_____. A woman often takes her husband's family name when she 13_____.

The earliest names in this country belong to American Indians, or Native 14_____. The family names of Native Americans today 15_____ show their closeness to nature. Two examples 16_____ Eva Whitecloud and John Littlehorse.

In Vietnam, family names come first 17_____ shows the importance of the family's ancestors. Nguyen Van Nam is a 18_____ boy. Nguyen is his family name. About half the 19_____ in Vietnam have the family name Nguyen.

Hispanic 20_____ have three parts. The first name is the "given" name. 21_____ first boy in the family 22_____ has the same given name as his father. The middle name is the father's 23_____ name. The last name is the mother's family name. 24_____ the last name isn't used. Luis Reyes Garcia is 25_____ Guatemala. His father's name is Luis Reyes Gonzalez. His 26_____ name is Maria Elena Garcia de Reyes.

A nickname is 27_____ name for a person. Sometimes a person's nickname is just a 28_____ form of the name. In the U.S., Tom is a 29_____ for Thomas. Liz is a nickname 30_____ Elizabeth.

Sometimes a nickname describes a person. 31_____ with red hair might be called "Red." A tall person might be known as "Stretch." 32_____ famous people are known by their 33_____. Bruce Springsteen, the singer, is called "The Boss." "Magic" Johnson is a basketball 34_____ . Where do you think their nicknames came 35_____?

Language Exercise

1. To fill gap 1 you can use either a singular or plural noun. Which is better? Why?

2. To fill gap 4 do you need a masculine or feminine pronoun? Which is better?

3. To fill gap 6 you need a noun with an apostrophe('s) to show possession. Which noun will you use?

4. Should the verb you use to complete gap 13 have an 's' or not? Why?

5. To fill gap 31 you could use *Someone* or *Somebody*. Is there any difference between these words?

Comprehension Exercise

1. Why do some parents in Africa wait for a few years before they name their children?

2. Why do family names come first in Vietnam?

3. Explain why Hispanic names usually have three parts.

4. What is the reason that many American Indian names show closeness to nature?

5. Where do the nicknames of the famous people in the passage come from?

Composition Exercise

Write an introductory or topic sentence for a paragraph about names. Use the answers to the comprehension questions in the previous exercise to help you to complete the paragraph. Feel free to leave out any sentence that doesn't seem to fit in your paragraph. You may need to add some sentences of your own. You may have to rearrange the sentences and find ways to connect them. If you have access to a computer and a word-processing program, you will find it easier to complete this exercise.

Vocabulary Review Exercise

Complete the following sentences with one of the words from the vocabulary list at the beginning of the unit. You may have to change the form of the word.

1. If you can't reach the top shelf, either stand on your toes and _____ or get a ladder.

2. It's very important to _____ a good name for a new product.

3. People from Asia usually have more respect for their _____ than people from the West do.

4. When you move to a new country, learning the new _____ may be as difficult as learning the new language.

5. Fresh flowers are so _____ that you must handle them very carefully.

6. The wedding _____ was held in the church; the reception was held in a park.

Topics for Discussion or Writing

1. What does your name mean and how did you get it? Do you like your name? If you could change your name, what would you want to be called?

2. When a woman marries should she keep her own name or take her husband's name? Explain why.

3. What do you think about nicknames? Would you call a stranger by his or her nickname? Why? What nickname would you give yourself if you don't have one?

4. Do you think new immigrants should change their names? Why?

5. What is the funniest name you've ever heard? Why do you think it is so funny?

Young People from Around the World at Newcomer High School in San Francisco, USA

UNIT 2

Coming to America

Before you begin trying to find a good word to fill in the gaps in the cloze passage, think about the following questions: Are you a new immigrant? Are there many new immigrants in your neighborhood? Where do they come from? Why do people decide to go and live in a new country? You might like to discuss these questions with your teacher and the whole class or with one or two classmates. You could also write the answer to these questions in a journal. As this unit is based on interviews, note that it is written in spoken English.

Dictionary Exercise

The passage, **Coming to America,** is about new immigrants coming to the United States. Some of the words in the passage may be difficult for you because they have more than one meaning. Read through a list of these words with their dictionary definitions. Try to predict which definition is most correct for a passage about new immigrants.

a. to **force** [VERB] *North American* /fɔrs/ *British* /fɔ:s/
   i.   to do something by force; compel
   ii. to break open, into, or through by force
   iii. to take by force; extort
   iv. to impose as by force

b. **military** [ADJECTIVE] *North American* /'milə,teri/ *British* /'milə,tri/
   i.   of, for, or done by soldiers
   ii. of, for, or fit for war
   iii. of the army

c. to **shave** [VERB] *North American* /seiv/ *British* /ʃeiv/
   i.   to cut away thin slices or sections from
   ii. a) to cut off (hair) at the surface of the skin
        b) to cut the hair to the surface of (the face)
   iii. to barely touch in passing; graze

d. **smart** [ADJECTIVE] *North American* /smart/ *British* /smɑːt/
   i.   to feel distress or irritation
   ii. intelligent; clever
   iii. neat; trim
   iv. stylish

After you have completed the cloze passage, go back to these words. Did you predict the correct definition of the word? You might like to compare your choice with other students in your class. If you don't agree, check your answer with your teacher. You will have another exercise in this unit in which you will be asked to use these words.

Coming to America

AHMAD MUMTAZ

"My father's friend said the military was coming to get us. So we left in the middle of the night," says Ahmad. Ahmad and his family were forced to 1_____ their home in Afghanistan. 2_____ country was at war. They traveled by car to Pakistan. 3_____ trip took six days.

"4_____ we waited four or five years for permission to 5_____ the U.S.," he says. "We came because my parents wanted 6_____ to have a better education. We 7_____ relatives here."

Ahmad spoke two 8_____ in Afghanistan, Persian and Pushtu. He learned a 9_____ language, Urdu, in Pakistan. Now he is studying English. Ahmad and his family hope to 10_____ to Afghanistan someday. "We plan 11_____ finish studying here. We'll go back when 12_____ safe," he says.

YAFFA TEVDIDIISHVILI

"I thought there would be people with strange haircuts — with purple hair and shaved heads," says Yaffa. Yaffa and her family 13_____ to the U.S. two years 14_____. They said good-bye to relatives and friends in Israel. "It was not easy to leave. I miss many 15_____," says Yaffa.

Some of Yaffa's relatives came to 16_____ U.S. many years ago. "My uncle in the U.S. 17_____ us come here," she says. "18_____ took time to save money and prepare the papers."

Yaffa has **19**_____ friends here. She enjoys being with American

teenagers and **20**_____ English. She is also learning Spanish. After Yaffa

completes her education, **21**_____ plans to go **22**_____ to Israel.

"It's strange here," she says. "Sometimes **23**_____ afraid to go outside

because I hear about all the crime. **24**_____ feel that Israel is my home."

SOYUN KIM

Soyun came to the U.S. with her mother and older sister in 1988. Her

father stayed in Korea. "It was hard to leave my **25**_____ and my father,

26_____ I have a lot of relatives here," says Soyun. "**27**_____ uncle

helped us get visas to come to the U.S. When we arrived, we

28_____ with my aunt."

Soyun and **29**_____ sister came to the U.S. to get a better

education. "It's very **30**_____ to go to college in Korea," she says.

"**31**_____ are not many colleges there. To go to college, you have to

32_____ very smart, the best."

In Korea, Soyun lived in a small **33**_____. Now she

34_____ in a large city. It has been a big change for her.

"**35**_____ different from the American kids, but I'm different

36_____ my friends in Korea, too. I'm in the middle," she says. "I'll go

back to **37**_____ to visit, but not to live." Soyun wants to

38_____ in the U.S. and become **39**_____ T.V. reporter "like

Connie Chung."

Language Exercise

1. Which verb should you use to fill gap 1: **live** or **leave?** Why do some students confuse these words?

2. Gap 3 needs to be filled with an article. Why do you need to use the definite article?

3. Do you fill gap 12 with **it's** or **its?** Can you explain why?

4. Gap 20 needs to be filled with a gerund (a word ending with -*ing*). Which word will you choose?

5. Which tense should you use for gap 28? Why?

Comprehension Exercise

1. Why did Ahmad and his family leave Afghanistan?

2. Are they planning to return to their country?

3. What did Yaffa think she would find in the U.S.?

4. Is she planning to stay in the U.S.?

5. Why did Soyun come to the U.S.?

Composition Exercise

Write an introductory or topic sentence for a paragraph about new immigrants to the United States. Use the answers to the comprehension questions in the previous exercise to help you to complete the paragraph. Feel free to leave out any sentence that doesn't seem to fit in your paragraph. You may need to add some sentences of your own. You may have to rearrange the sentences and find ways to connect them. If you have access to a computer and a word-processing program, you will find it easier to complete this exercise.

Vocabulary Exercise

Complete the following sentences with one of the words from the vocabulary list at the beginning of the unit. You may have to change the form of the word.

1. Many young boys can't wait for the day when they begin to _____ every day.

2. _____ students usually get the highest grades.

3. Some young people like to wear _____ uniforms even though they are not in the army.

4. In some countries young people are _____ to serve in the army even if they don't want to.

Topics for Discussion or Writing

1. Why did you come to this country? Were your reasons the same or different from the young people you have just read about?

2. What are some of the problems new immigrants have in adjusting to a new country?

3. If you went back to your old country, what do you think you would find strange or different?

4. Some people believe that the reason that the United States is so powerful and so popular as a new country for people from other countries, is because it is basically a country of immigrants. What do you think about this idea?

James Edward Olmos as Jaime Escalante in "Stand and Deliver"

It's No Act

Before you begin trying to find a word to fill the gaps, think about the following questions: What do you know about Latinos (Hispanics)? Do you like to see movies that try to teach you how to live? Can you name a movie of this kind? Do you believe that your national origin has anything to do with your success at school? Why do some students do better at school than others? You might like to discuss these questions with your teacher and the whole class or with one or two classmates. You could also write the answer to these questions in a journal. This passage is an article from a magazine for young people.

Dictionary Exercise

The passage, **It's No Act,** is about a movie star and one of the films he acts in. Some of the words in the passage may be difficult for you because they have more than one meaning. Read through a list of these words with their dictionary definitions. Try to predict which definition is most correct for a passage about a movie star.

a. **cause** [NOUN] *North American /kɔz/ British /kɔːz/*
   i.   anything producing an effect or result
   ii. a reason or motive for producing an effect
   iii. any objective or movement that people are interested in or support
   iv. a case to be decided in court

b. to **play** [VERB] *North American /pleɪ/ British /pleɪ/*
   i.   to move lightly, rapidly, etc.
   ii.   to engage in recreation
   iii. to take part in a game or sport
   iv.   to perform on a musical instrument
   v.   to give out sounds
   vi.   to act in a specified way
   vii. to act in a drama

c. to **raise** [VERB] *North American* /reiz/ *British* /reɪz/
   i.   to cause to rise; lift
   ii. to construct; build
   iii. to increase in size, amount, degree and/or intensity
   iv. to provoke; inspire
   v. to present for consideration (raise a question)
   vi. to collect (an army, money, etc.)
   vii. to cause to grow
   viii.to end (a siege)
   ix. to cause to grow (children)

d. **tough** [ADJECTIVE] *North American* /təf/ *British* /tʌf/
   i.   that will bend without tearing or breaking
   ii. not easily cut or chewed (tough steak)
   iii. strong; hardy
   iv. stubborn
   v. brutal or rough
   vi. very difficult; laborious

After you have completed the cloze passage, go back to these words. Did you predict the correct definition of the word? You might like to compare your choice with other students in your class. If you don't agree, check your answer with your teacher. You will have another exercise in this unit in which you will be asked to use these words.

Happiness is . . . a Caribbean Cruise

It's Saturday afternoon and you are in the cruise capital of the world –

Miami – and you thought the day would never come!

1_____ feel the excitement as you enter the new port area and

2_____ the laughter of fellow passengers and begin to experience the

happy feeling of the long awaited 3_____.

You're quickly checked 4_____, your dining seating is already

arranged, and your luggage on 5_____ way to your cabin. It seems like

you just got here and yet you 6_____ already aboard and ready to sail. If

your friends 7_____ see you 8_____.

And there you are on deck happily waving 9_____ as your ship

slowly leaves the pier and gains momentum toward the Caribbean cruise

10_____ always dreamed of taking.

You look around as the Miami skyline disappears and 11_____ your

fellow passengers 12_____ by. They're of all ages, yet they all share the

same exciting anticipation of a 13_____ cruise.

14_____ is smiling, both passengers and crew, and before you

know it you are 15_____ friends for a lifetime. 16_____ with

whom you'll share your vacation, your shipboard life and the pleasure of your

time 17_____ in the friendly Caribbean 18_____.

Vocabulary Review Exercise

Complete the following sentences with one of the words from the vocabulary list at the beginning of this unit. You may have to change the form of the word.

1. We walked down to the _____ to see the ships.

2. Does a falling body gain _____?

3. At most hotels you can't _____ in until noon.

4. Very often the _____ of a special event, is the best part of it.

5. Many cities are established because they are on the ocean and serve as _____.

6. Before you look for a job, it helps if you have _____ experience in the field.

7. Every year they go for a _____ to explore a different part of the world.

8. I have _____ great pleasure in my study of music and art.

Topics for Discussion or Writing

1. What are some of the advantages and disadvantages of a vacation on a ship?

2. Write a letter to a travel agent making enquiries about a cruise you would like to take.

3. Find some advertisements for vacations. Study them and try to decide if they are true.

4. Imagine that you are taking this cruise. Write a postcard to a friend describing your feelings as the ship left Miami.

5. Describe the most unusual or interesting vacation you ever had.

Language Exercise

1. Suggest at least three words that are possible for gap 3.

2. Which of the following words is correct for gap 5: *it's* or *its?* Why?

3. For gap 7 which is better *could* or *can?* Why?

4. Consider the words *goodbye* and *farewell* for gap 9. Which is preferable and why?

5. Find at least three words that can be used to fill gap 12.

6. Which form of the verb should be used in gap 15: *making, made,* or *makes?*

7. Is the word *friends* better than the word *people* to fill gap 16? Why?

8. The present progressive is used quite often in this passage. Why is that?

Comprehension Exercise

1. Which city do most cruise ships leave from?

2. Describe some of the arrangements that are made when the passengers arrive for their cruise.

3. Describe the mood of the passengers as they leave for their cruise.

4. What kind of things do passengers do to spend their time on such vacations?

Composition Exercise

Write an introductory or topic sentence for a paragraph about a cruise. Use the answers to the comprehension questions in the previous exercise to help you to complete the paragraph. Feel free to leave out any sentence that doesn't seem to fit your paragraph. You will need to add some sentences of your own. You may need to rearrange the sentences and find ways to connect them. If you have access to a computer and a word-processing program, you will find it easier to complete this exercise.

Vocabulary Review Exercise

Complete the following sentences with one of the words from the vocabulary list at the beginning of the unit. You may have to change the form of the word.

1. The dog's not hungry. It can't stop eating because it's so _____.

2. We couldn't eat the food as it was so _____.

3. Students who are absent without an _____ will be dropped.

4. The music was so powerful it blew my _____.

5. My grandmother always used to give me _____ advice.

6. Elvis began to sing and a crowd soon _____ around him.

7. There have been _____ changes recently in what was the USSR.

8. Close _____ cannot marry according to the law.

9. Turn around and _____ me. Did you do it?

10. She could feel her heart _____ after winning the race.

11. My teacher told me to _____ the violin every day.

Topics for Discussion or Writing

1. Which joke did you like best? Why?

2. Which joke did you think was not funny at all. Can you explain why?

3. Translate a joke from your first language into English.

4. Write down the best English joke you know.

It's No Act

Edward James Olmos is a tough cop on television. He is Martin Castillo on *Miami Vice*. Now Olmos is in a movie called *Stand and Deliver*. In this movie he still plays a tough guy. But this time, he's not a 1_____, he plays a teacher.

The movie is about a real 2_____, Jaime Escalante. Escalante 3_____ math. In the school where 4_____ teaches, most of the students are Asian and Hispanic.

5_____ Escalante first started teaching, 6_____ of his students were failing. But he showed 7_____ that they can do well if they 8_____. Now his high school is one of the 9_____ in Los Angeles.

Olmos comes 10_____ the same neighborhood where Jaime Escalante teaches. Many 11_____ Escalante's students are Mexican-Americans. So 12_____ Olmos.

Olmos is like the teacher 13_____ plays. He spends a lot of 14_____ helping people. He raised money 15_____ survivors of the 1985 earthquake in Mexico City. He speaks out for Hispanic causes. And 16_____ refuses to act in films that make Hispanics 17_____ bad.

In his free time, Olmos visits teens in youth centers. He has a special

message for young **18**_____: "If you work **19**_____, stick to it, and

practice, **20**_____ succeed."

    That's the same message Escalante sends **21**_____ students. The

lives of both Escalante and Olmos prove **22**_____ message is true.

Language Exercise

1. Gap 5 must be filled by a **wh** word. Which one is it?

2. Gap 6 can be filled with one of these words: **many, all** or **most.** Which word do you prefer? Why?

3. Gap 12 should be filled by one form of the verb '**to be.**' Which tense should you use? Explain.

4. In gap 14 you could say that Olmos spends '**time**' or '**money.**' Which makes more sense to you?

5. Gap 20 needs to be filled by a contraction. Which two words make up the contraction?

Comprehension Exercise

1. In which movies can you see Edward Olmos?

2. What do you know about Jaime Escalante?

3. What do Olmos and Escalante have in common?

4. What kind of volunteer work does Olmos do?

5. What advice does he have for young people?

Composition Exercise

Write an introductory or topic sentence for a paragraph about Jaime Escalante. Use the answers to the comprehension questions in the previous exercise to help you to complete the paragraph. Feel free to leave out any sentence that doesn't seem to fit in your paragraph. You may need to add some sentences of your own. You may have to rearrange the sentences and find ways to connect them. If you have access to a computer and a word-processing program, you will find it easier to complete this exercise.

Vocabulary Review Exercise

Complete the following sentences with one of the words from the vocabulary list at the beginning of the unit. You may have to change the form of the word.

1. Most people have problems finding the right way to _____ their children.

2. When you were in the high school drama production, which role did you _____?

3. It's _____ trying to make a decision about your future. You have so many options.

4. The Red Cross helps people in many countries. It's a good _____ to give money to.

Topics for Discussion or Writing

1. Have you seen the movie *Stand and Deliver*? If you have, what did you think about it? If you have not seen it, ask your teacher to show the movie to your class. Have you seen any other movies with a message? Explain.

2. Some people seem to believe that Asian immigrants are better students than Latinos. Do you agree? Why or why not?

3. What do you think about the message that Olmos and Escalante give to young people?

4. Can you think of a book, a movie, or a television program that changed your life? Explain.

Singing "La Bamba" made Ritchie Valens an Overnight Success

The American Dream

Before you begin trying to find a suitable word to fill in the gaps in the cloze passage, think about the following questions: What does "The American Dream" mean to you? How can a person become rich and famous in the United States? Have you heard about a movie called *La Bamba*? Have you ever heard the song "La Bamba?" Is it important to be in the right place at the right time in order to succeed? What are some other ways to succeed? You might like to discuss these questions with your teacher and the whole class or with one or two classmates. You could also write the answer to these questions in a journal. Notice that this unit is an interview so that the language used is spoken not written.

Dictionary Exercise

The passage, **The American Dream,** is about success. Some of the words in the passage may be difficult for you because they have more than one meaning. Read through a list of these words with their dictionary definitions. Try to predict which definition is most correct for a passage about achieving the American Dream.

a. **gentle** [ADJECTIVE] *North American* /ˈdʒentəl/ *British* /ˈdʒentl/
   i.   of the upper classes
   ii. refined, courteous
   iii. generous, kind
   iv. tame (i.e., a dog)
   v.   not harsh or rough, mild
   vi. gradual (a gentle slope)

b. **goal** [NOUN] *North American* /ɡoul/ *British* /ɡəʊl/
   i.   the place at which a race or trip is ended
   ii. an end that one strives to attain
   iii. in some games
        a) the place over or into which the ball or puck must go to score
        b) the score made

c. **morals** [NOUN] *North American* /ˈmɔrəlz/ *British* /ˈmɑrəlz/
   i.   a moral lesson taught by a fable or event (singular)
   ii. principles or standards with respect to right or wrong in conduct

d. **nature** [NOUN] *North American* /ˈneɪtʃər/ *British* /ˈneɪtʃə(r)/
   i.   the essential quality of a thing: essence
   ii. inherent tendencies of a person
   iii kind; type
   iv. a) the entire physical universe
        b) the power and force that seems to regulate this

e. **opportunity** [NOUN] *North American* /ˌapərˈtunəti/ *British* /ˌapəˈtuːnətɪ/
   i.   a combination of circumstances favorable for a purpose
   ii. a good chance

f. **overnight** [ADVERB] *North American* /ˌouvərˈnait/ *British* /ˈəuvəˈnuɪt/
   i.   during the night
   ii. suddenly

g. **positive** [ADJECTIVE] *North American* /ˈpazətɪv/ *British* /ˈpazətɪv/
   i.   definitely set; explicit
   ii.   having the mind set; confident
   iii. showing agreement; affirmation
   iv.   constructive
   v.   regarding having real existence
   vi.   based on facts

h. to **treat** [VERB] *North American* /trit/ *British* /triːt/
   i.   to discuss terms (with)
   ii.   to speak or write (of)
   iii. to deal with (a subject) in writing music, etc., in a specified manner
   iv.   to act toward (someone or something) in a specified manner
   v.   to pay for the food of (another)
   vi.   to subject to some process or chemical
   vii. to give medical care to

After you have completed the cloze passage, go back to these words. Did you predict the correct definition of the word? You might like to compare your choice with other students in your class. If you don't agree, check your answer with your teacher. You will have another exercise in this unit in which you will be asked to use these words.

The American Dream

To many people, Ritchie Valens' life was the American Dream come true. He came from a poor family. But he worked hard – and he became a success. *U.S. Express* spoke with Lou Diamond Phillips, the actor who played Ritchie. Here is what he told us.

U.S. EXPRESS: Ritchie Valens became an overnight success with 1_____ song "La Bamba." Did the same thing happen to you 2_____ the movie?

PHILLIPS: Just like Ritchie, I was in the 3_____ place at the right time. But it didn't happen overnight for 4_____. I worked many years to reach this goal.

U.S. EXPRESS: 5_____ you and Ritchie alike?

PHILLIPS: Yes, I think 6_____. Ritchie had a sweet and gentle nature. And he 7_____ believed in himself. I'm like that 8_____. And, like Ritchie, I have big dreams.

U.S. EXPRESS: *La Bamba* is about Mexican-Americans. 9_____ this movie changed anything for Hispanics?

PHILLIPS: Yes, often, Hispanic actors have to 10_____ the bad guys in movies. **11**_____ the gang members. *La Bamba* was the first Hollywood

12_____ that shows a positive side of Hispanic life.

U.S. EXPRESS: 13_____ do you think people liked Ritchie and the movie

14_____ much?

PHILLIPS: They see in him a return to morals and good values. Ritchie

15_____ really a nice guy. He loved his family. He treated

16_____ the way he wanted to be treated – **17**_____ respect and

warmth. And, at age 17, he **18**_____ after the American Dream. He

wanted to be somebody. It **19**_____ just for the money.

U.S. EXPRESS: What is the "American **20**_____"? What does it mean to

you?

PHILLIPS: It means **21**_____ hard to get what you want. No one is going

to just hand things **22**_____ you.

U.S. EXPRESS: 23_____ do you think the American Dream means to

young people today?

PHILLIPS: 24_____ different now. Today, the American Dream is to own

more things – a bigger house, a better **25**_____.

U.S. EXPRESS: Is it harder for young people to 26_____ their personal dreams come true?

PHILLIPS: Much harder. There are still opportunities out 27_____. But life is not as simple as it 28_____. Now there are so many things to think about.

U.S. EXPRESS: 29_____ advice do you have for young people today?

PHILLIPS: Find out as 30_____ as you can about the thing you want to do. Believe 31_____ yourself and go after what you 32_____.

Language Exercise

1. Gap 1 must be completed with an article. Should you use *a* or *the?*

2. Is gap 8 filled with *to, two,* or *too?*

3. Gap 9 needs an auxiliary verb. Should you use *Did, Have, Has,* or *Had?*

4. Gap 11 is filled by a contraction. What are the two words that form the contraction?

5. To fill gap 24 should you use *its* or *it's?*

Comprehension Exercise

1. What was Ritchie Valens famous for?

2. What do Ritchie Valens and Lou Diamond Phillips have in common?

3. What kind of roles do most Mexican-Americans play in Hollywood movies?

4. What kind of person was Ritchie Valens?

5. What does the "American Dream" mean to Lou Diamond Phillips?

Composition Exercise

Write an introductory or topic sentence for a paragraph about Richie Valens and the American Dream. Use the answers to the comprehension questions in the previous exercise to help you to complete the paragraph. Feel free to leave out any sentence that doesn't seem to fit in your paragraph. You may need to add some sentences of your own. You may have to rearrange the sentences and find ways to connect them. If you have access to a computer and a word-processing program, you will find it easier to complete this exercise.

Vocabulary Review Exercise

Complete the following sentences with one of the words from the vocabulary list at the beginning of the unit. You may have to change the form of the word.

1. When you pick up the baby, be _____.

2. I'm always looking for _____ to teach my students grammar and vocabulary.

3. If you _____ people well, usually they will be good to you.

4. The test was _____. We're going to have a baby!

5. Nobody had ever heard of Madonna. Now everyone knows who she is. She was an _____ sensation.

6. Religious people generally worry about the _____ of young people. They are afraid that they will behave badly.

7. What are your immediate _____? Do you want to transfer to a university?

8. Scientists are very interested in the question of whether _____ or nurture are more important in the development of a person.

Topics for Discussion or Writing

1. What is your American Dream?

2. Did you see the movie *La Bamba?* What do you think about it? If you have not seen it, ask your teacher to show it to your class.

3. What would Jaime Escalante think about Ritchie Valens? What do you think of him?

4. Many popular singers died when they were very young. Do you know any others apart from Ritchie Valens? How did they die?

Mary Nguyen, Revlon's Most Unforgettable Woman of 1989

Mary Nguyen

Before you begin to write answers to the gaps in the next passage, think about the following questions: What do you think about beauty contests? How do people in Asia usually treat Amerasians? How do people in this country treat people who have mixed blood? Do Americans generally take such things as a home, food, education for granted? You might like like to discuss these questions with your teacher and the whole class or with one or two classmates. You could also write the answer to these questions in a journal. Notice that this passage is an interview so the language used is spoken rather than written.

Dictionary Exercise

The passage, **Mary Nguyen,** is about Mary Nguyen, a new immigrant who won a beauty contest. Some of the words in the passage may be difficult for you because they have more than one meaning. Read through a list of these words with their dictionary definitions. Try to predict which definition is most correct for a passage about a beauty queen.

a. to **adjust** [VERB] *North American* /əˈdʒəst/ *British* /əˈdʒʌst/
   i.   to change so as to fit
   ii. to regulate (a watch)
   iii. to settle rightly
   iv. to decide the amount to be paid in settling (an insurance claim)

b. **dust** [NOUN] *North American* /dəst/ *British* /dʌst/
   i.   powdery earth or any finely powdered matter
   ii. earth
   iii. disintegrated mortal remains
   iv. anything worthless

c. **overcome** [VERB] *North American* /ˌouvərˈkəm/ *British* /ˌəuvəˈkʌm/
   i.   to get the better of in competition
   ii. to master, surmount, or overwhelm

d. to **stick** [VERB] *North American* /stɪk/ *British* /stɪk/
  i.   to pierce, as with a pointed instrument
  ii. to thrust
  iii. to attach as by gluing or pinning
  iv. to obstruct or detain
  v.   (colloquial) to put or set
  vi. (colloquial) to puzzle or baffle

After you have completed the cloze passage, go back to these words. Did you predict the correct definition of the word? You might like to compare your choice with other students in your class. If you don't agree, check your answer with your teacher. You will have another exercise in this unit in which you will be asked to use these words.

Mary Nguyen

Mary Nguyen is a college student. She won Revlon's "Most Unforgettable Woman of 1989" contest. Mary's boyfriend heard about the contest and persuaded her to enter. Mary didn't think she'd win. "I'm Amerasian," she says, "not blond or all-American." But she **1**_____ an essay telling why she's "unforgettable." In her essay, she wrote: "In Vietnam, I **2**_____ considered a dishonor to my country. To overcome this, I **3**_____ to develop a stronger sense of myself. **4**_____ cannot rely on looks alone."

U.S. EXPRESS: What are your memories **5**_____ Vietnam?

MARY: I was only five **6**_____ I left, but I felt different from other people, I looked **7**_____, and people would point me out. I was a "child of the dust." In Vietnamese, that **8**_____ someone who's **9**_____ than the dust you walk on. People use the term **10**_____ describe Amerasians.

U.S. EXPRESS: Do you know anything **11**_____ your father?

MARY: I have some information that will help **12**_____ find out more about him. I don't know if **13**_____ even alive, but I think I'll look for him when I get **14**_____ of college. When I was younger I was afraid he

15_____ accept me, or that he had his own family. **16**_____ worst fear was that he died.

U.S. EXPRESS: **17**_____ did you get out of Vietnam?

MARY: My mom and I were on vacation in Saigon. We lived in Da Nang. It was **18**_____ the fall of Saigon and everything was **19**_____ – the roads, the airport, the train stations. We were stuck in Saigon, and **20**_____ was getting a lot worse. My mom **21**_____ she had to get me to the United States. She found **22**_____ about an American adoption agency that wanted Amerasian children.

U.S. EXPRESS: **23**_____ was it like coming to the U.S.?

MARY: It was traumatic. I **24**_____ to learn a new language, and adjust to a **25**_____ family and a new country. After five months, my mom **26**_____ to the U.S. and I went to live **27**_____ her. But when she gave me up in Vietnam, she **28**_____ she'd never see me again.

U.S. EXPRESS: **29**_____ it hard to be an Amerasian living in the U.S.?

MARY: **30**_____ elementary school and junior high, it was **31**_____ to be accepted. Since I was from Vietnam, kids **32**_____ say, "Oh, you're Vietcong. You're the enemy." In high school and college,

33_____ were more accepting.

U.S. EXPRESS: What are your future **34**_____?

MARY: I want to go to law school and become a representative for Amerasians

and Vietnamese people. And I **35**_____ to go back to Vietnam and

36_____ in any way I can.

U.S. EXPRESS: Is **37**_____ anything you'd like to say to our readers?

MARY: **38**_____ funny, but I feel fortunate coming from another country.

I **39**_____ take things for granted. People here don't understand

40_____ it's like to be in a country at war, or to be poor. In this country,

41_____ so much. The United States is great, but it's important to

remember who you are and where you come from.

Language Exercise

1. Gap 4 can be filled with either **you** or **one**. Which is better and why?

2. You need a preposition to fill gap 5. Is there a choice, or must you use only one word?

3. Gap 13 needs to be filled with a contraction. Which two words make up this contraction?

4. What kind of question word do you need to fill gap 17: **How** or **When?**

5. Gap 22 needs a preposition. Which word usually goes with **find?**

Comprehension Exercise

1. Why did Mary Nguyen enter the beauty competition?

2. Why was she not treated well in Vietnam?

3. What did her mother think when she sent Mary to the U.S.?

4. How did the children at school in the U.S. treat her?

5. What kind of advice does she give to us?

Composition Exercise

Write an introductory or topic sentence for a paragraph about Mary Nguyen. Use the answers to the comprehension questions in the previous exercise to help you to complete the paragraph. Feel free to leave out any sentence that doesn't seem to fit in your paragraph. You may need to add some sentences of your own. You may have to rearrange the sentences and find ways to connect them. If you have access to a computer and a word-processing program, you will find it easier to complete this exercise.

Vocabulary Exercise

Complete the following sentences with one of the words from the vocabulary list at the beginning of the unit. You may have to change the form of the word.

1. One of the most famous American folk-songs is "We Shall _____."

2. You can't eat that chocolate now. It fell in the _____ and it's dirty.

3. I can't open the drawer – it's _____.

4. New immigrants often find it difficult to _____ to a new country.

Topics For Discussion or Writing

1. Would you take part in a beauty competition? Do they exist in the country where you were born?

2. How do most Americans treat people with different color skins? Give some examples.

3. If you could met Mary Nguyen, what kind of questions would you ask her?

Remembering My Teacher

When No One is Looking

Before you begin trying to find a good word to fill in the gaps in this cloze passage, think about the following questions: If you were a teacher and you noticed that your pupils were cheating in a test, what would you do? If you found a purse in a public place, what would you do with it? If you are given extra change in a store, what would you do with it? You might like to discuss these questions with your teacher and the whole class or with one or two classmates. You could also write the answer to these questions in a journal. This passage is a personal essay. It is the kind of style you should try to use when you write a composition about something personal.

Dictionary Exercise

The passage, **When No One is Looking,** is about twelve third-grade boys who cheated on an arithmetic test. Their teacher caught them and gave them an unusual punishment. Some of the words in the passage may be difficult for you because they have more than one meaning. Read through a list of these words with their dictionary definitions. Try to predict which definition is most correct in a passage about cheating.

a. **character** [NOUN] *North American* /ˈkærɪktər/ *British* /ˈkærəktə(r)/
   i. nature; features or qualities that make a country or person different from others
   ii. moral strength; reputation
   iii. person in a novel or play
   iv. odd or unusual person
   v. letter, sign, or mark used in a system of writing or printing

b. to **compose** [VERB] *North American* /kəmˈpouz/ *British* /kəmˈpəʊz/
   i. make up
   ii. put together
   iii. set up type
   iv. get under control

c. **confidence** [NOUN] *North American* /ˈkɑnfədəns/ *British* /ˈkɑnfɪdəns/
   i. expecting something to be kept secret
   ii. secret
   iii. belief in oneself or others

d. a **decision** [NOUN] *North American* /dɪˈsɪʒən/ *British* /dɪˈsɪʒn/
   i. deciding, judging
   ii. result of this; settlement of a question
   iii. ability to decide and act

e. to **guide** [VERB] *North American* /gaɪd/ *British* /gaɪd/
   i. to point out the way, lead
   ii. to direct or control

f. to **mark** [VERB] *North American* /mark/ *British* /ma·k/
   i. to make a mark on something
   ii. indicate with a mark or visible sign
   iii. give marks to; grade
   iv. pay attention to

g. to **measure** [VERB] *North American* /meʒər/ *British* /ˈmeʒə(r)/
   i. to find the size, extent, volume, etc.
   ii. have as a measurement
   iii. give or mark a measured quantity

h. **personal** [ADJECTIVE] *North American* /ˈpərsənəl/ *British* /ˈpɜˈsənl/
   i. private; individual; of a particular person
   ii. done or made by a person himself or herself
   iii. done for or directed to a particular person
   iv. of the body
   v. of or about a person

i. to **remain** [VERB] *North American* /rɪˈmeɪn/ *British* /rɪˈmeɪn/
   i. be still present after a part has gone or been taken away
   ii. continue in some place or condition

j. **respect** [NOUN] /rɪˈspekt/
   i. honor; high opinion
   ii. consideration; regard
   iii. reference; relation to
   iv. detail; particular aspect
   v. regards; polite greetings

k. **single** [ADJECTIVE] *North American* /ˈsɪŋgəl/ *British* /ˈsɪŋgl/
   i. one only
   ii. not married
   iii. for the use of, used for, done by, a person

1. a **tool** [NOUN] *North American* /tul/ *British* /tu:l/
    i. instrument held in the hand(s) and used by workers
    ii. person used by another for dishonest purposes

After you have completed the cloze passage, go back to these words. Did you predict the correct definition of the word? You might like to compare your choice with other students in your class. If you don't agree, check your answer with your teacher. You will have another exercise in this unit in which you will be asked to use these words.

When No One is Looking

"The measure of a man's real character is what he would do if he knew he would never be found out." THOMAS MACAULAY

Some thirty years ago, in a public school on New York's Lower East side, a Mrs. O'Neill gave an arithmetic test to her third-grade class. When the papers were marked she discovered that twelve boys had written the same answer to an arithmetic problem.

There is 1_____ really new about cheating in exams. Perhaps that was why Mrs. O'Neill didn't even 2_____ anything about it.

3_____ only asked the twelve boys to remain after class.

They 4_____ with fear in their hearts, for they knew why Mrs. O'Neill wanted to see them. They were 5_____ but only in part.

Mrs. O' Neill asked no 6_____. She said nothing. She gave out no punishment.

7_____ she was alone with the 8_____ pupils, Mrs. O' Neill wrote on the blackboard the above twenty 9_____ words, together with the name of the great man who composed 10_____. She then ordered them to 11_____ these words into their copy-books one hundred times.

12_____ don't know about the other eleven boys. Speaking for

13_____ I can say: it was the most important single 14_____ of my

life.

My life happens to have 15_____ lived up to now in a

16_____ of uncertainty, danger, and fear. It is good, of 17_____, to

learn from history that all times have been full of fear, uncertainty and

18_____, but a man wants more than 19_____, he wants tools to

work with, yardsticks to measure by.

Thirty years after being introduced to Macaulay's words, they

20_____ seem to me one of the best yardsticks I have 21_____

met. 22_____ because they give us a way to measure others, but

23_____ they give us a way to measure 24_____.

Few of us are asked to 25_____ great decisions about nations going

to war 26_____ armies going to battle. But all of us are called

27_____ daily to make a great many personal decisions. 28_____

the purse, found in the 29_____, be put into a pocket or turned over to

the 30_____? Should the extra change received at the grocer's be

forgotten or returned?

31_____ will know. Nobody 32_____ you. But you have to

live with yourself, and it is always better to live with someone you

33_____, because respect develops confidence, and 34_____ is a

great weapon, especially in times of fear, 35_____, and danger.

Language Exercise

1. In gap 8 there are a number of possibilities. You need a descriptive word, an adjective, such as *guilty, dishonest, fearful,* or *twelve.* Which one do you think is most suitable?

2. In gap 10 you should have written the word *them.* Why do you need to use the plural form here?

3. Explain why it would be better to use the word *copy* in gap 11 than the word *write?*

4. The possibilities for gap 14 are *event, happening, day,* or *lesson.* Which do you think is best, and why?

5. What does the word *that* refer to in gap 19?

Comprehension Exercise

1. How old was the author when the incident he describes happened to him?

2. Where was he living at the time?

3. Why do we need to measure ourselves? What important lesson did he learn?

4. What does the author say about history?

5. What kind of personal decisions are we asked to make every day?

Composition Exercise

Write an introductory or topic sentence for a paragraph about how the author learned not to cheat. Use the answers to the comprehension questions in the previous exercise to help you to complete the paragraph. Feel free to leave out any sentence that doesn't seem to fit in your paragraph. You may need to add some sentences of your own. You may have to rearrange the sentences and find ways to connect them. If you have access to a computer and a word-processing program, you will find it easier to complete this exercise.

Vocabulary Review Exercise

Complete the following sentences with one of the words from the vocabulary list at the beginning of the unit. You may have to change the form of the word.

1. Mother Teresa is a woman of noble and fine _____.

2. You need to have _____ in yourself so that you can perform well.

3. My _____ affairs are none of your business.

4. One of the pupils asked their teacher if she had _____ their tests.

5. I've been offered two jobs but I haven't reached a _____ about which one to accept.

6. Carpenters use special _____ such as hammers, saws, and chisels.

7. If you don't work hard at school, you may have to _____ in the same class for two years.

8. Mozart, Beethoven, and Liszt were great European _____.

9. Many people rely on their religions to _____ them in making decisions.

10. It doesn't matter how much they pay you, if they don't _____ you, you'll never be happy in that job.

Topics for Discussion or Writing

1. What kind of qualities do people need to have in order for you to respect them?

2. Can you find any examples of sexist writing in the cloze passage? How would you change them to sound more fair?

3. Although the author of the passage states "She gave out no punishment," what Mrs. O' Neill did, in fact, is usually considered to be a punishment. What do you think?

4. Your teacher has given you a higher mark than you deserve because the marks have been added incorrectly. What would you do about it?

5. Imagine that you're due to have a major operation and you tell the patient in the next bed the name of your surgeon. To your horror, the other patient tells you that surgeon had cheated all the way through medical school. How would you feel and what would you do?

Elephant Escapes from the Circus!

A Letter to the Family

Before you begin trying to find a good word to fill in the gaps in this cloze passage, think about the following questions: What kind of relationship did you have with your grandparents? What kind of things did you do with them? What do you think about visiting the zoo or circus? You might like to discuss these questions with your teacher and the whole class or with one or two classmates. You could also write the answer to these questions in a journal. This unit is based on a personal letter. Notice the way the address and the beginning and ending of the letter are written. When you write a personal letter, you should use a similar form.

Dictionary Exercise

The passage, **A Letter to the Family,** is a letter from a grandmother to her children. She describes a visit to the circus and what happened there. Some of the words in the passage may be difficult for you because they have more than one meaning. Read through a list of these words with their dictionary definitions. Try to predict which definition is most correct in a letter describing what happened at the circus.

a. **apologetic** [ADJECTIVE] *North American* /əpalə'dʒetɪk/ *British* /əˌpalə'dʒetɪk/
    i. making an apology
    ii. excusing a fault or failure

b. to **assume** [VERB] *North American* /ə'sum / *British* /ə'sjuːm /
    i. take for granted without proof
    ii. undertake; begin to govern
    iii. take on; pretend to have

c. to **assure** [VERB] *North American* /ə'ʃur/ *British* /ə'ʃuə(r)/
    i. say positively with confidence
    ii. cause a person to be sure, feel certain

d. **concern** [NOUN] *North American* /kən'sərn/ *British* /kən'sɛːn/
    i. relation or connection
    ii. business or undertaking
    iii. anxiety

e. to **disturb** [VERB] *North American* /dɪ'stərb / *British* /dɪ'stɛːb/
   i.   break the quiet, calm, peace or order of
   ii. put out of the right or usual position

f. **explanation** [NOUN] *North American* /ˌeksplə'neɪʃən/ *British* /eksplə'neɪʃn/
   i.   process of explaining
   ii. statements, facts or circumstances that explain

g. **incident** [NOUN] *North American* /'ɪnsədənt/ *British* /'ɪnsɪdənt/
   i.   event, especially one of less importance than others
   ii. happening which attracts general attention

h. to **involve** [VERB] *North American* /ɪn'vɑlv/ *British* /ɪn'vɑlv/
   i.   cause a person to be caught or mixed up in trouble
   ii.   devote much time and attention to
   iii. require
   iv.   take in, include

i. a **member** [NOUN] *North American* /'membər/ *British* /'membə(r)/
   i.   person belonging to a group or society
   ii. part of a human or animal body

j. **naturally** [ADVERB] *North American* /'nætʃ(ə)rəli/ *British* /'nætʃrəlɪ/
   i.   by nature
   ii.   of course, as might be expected
   iii. without artificial help
   iv.   without exaggeration or help

k. to **request** [VERB] /rɪ'kwest/
   i.   asking or being asked
   ii. something asked for

After you have completed the cloze passage, go back to these words. Did you predict the correct definition? You might like to compare your choice with other students in your class. If you don't agree, check with you teacher. You will have another exercise in this unit in which you will be asked to use these words.

A Letter to the Family

55 Shakespeare Road,
Greenside.

Saturday, June 13, 1992

My dear children,

It's hard to believe that I've been here for a month. The time passes so quickly and there's so much to do.

I've managed to see all the members of the family. I 1_____ as much time as I can with the children. Last week I 2_____ Mark and Michelle to the circus. 3_____ never been before as they live quite far from the nearest city and their parents 4_____ have time to drive them there. I 5_____ that's what grandmothers are for.

Susan 6_____ me her car – it's a brand-new red compact. We left early so as to make a day of 7_____. In the morning we 8_____ to the zoo and in the afternoon to the circus.

As 9_____ can imagine, the children were very excited. They loved everything. Mark 10_____ the wild animals the most interesting and Michelle is 11_____ to be an acrobat when she grows 12_____.

After we'd been there for about two hours we 13_____ an announcement over the loudspeaker. The owner of the Volkswagen number

PUR 727V 14_____ requested to come to the manager's office

15_____. Naturally, I didn't know the number of 16_____ car so I

left the children and went to the manager's office to 17_____ out if it was

our car.

The manager looked very upset and 18_____. No one else had

answered his call so I assumed correctly that it was Susan's car. 19_____

that I'd left the lights on, or parked in 20_____ way, I wasn't

21_____ concerned, but I didn't know why the manager looked so

disturbed. He began to 22_____ what happened and it took me some

time to understand 23_____ confused explanation.

24_____ appears that the elephants are trained to sit on red boxes.

One of the elephants 25_____ escaped and when it saw the

26_____ red car it promptly sat on 27_____! As you can imagine

the car looked a mess. One side was squashed 28_____ but it was still

possible to drive. The manager assured 29_____ that the circus would

pay for the 30_____. He couldn't have been more apologetic.

The children were very 31_____ and giggled about the incident all

the way home. 32_____ before we got there, we 33_____ the

scene of a serious accident. About a mile 34_____ on a policeman

stopped us and asked if we'd 35_____ involved in the accident. I wish I had a 36_____ of his face when I told him what had happened

37_____ the car. I think he wanted to arrest me for drunken driving!

Fortunately the 38_____ were there to back me up. 39_____

are you managing without me? Please don't 40_____ to water my plants.

I'm planning to leave here 41_____ the end of the month.

My love to you all,

Mom

Language Exercise

1. In gap 1 you need to use a verb. Why should you use the simple present tense?

2. In gap 2 you also need a verb. Why should you use the simple past tense?

3. Gap 3 must be completed with **they'd.** What word does the **d** replace?

4. Gap 5 can be completed with one of these verbs: **suppose, guess, think,** or **imagine.** Which is the most suitable word, and why?

5. The words **you** and **one** can be used to fill gap 9. Which is better, and why?

6. Consider **is** and **was** to fill gap 14. Which is the correct one and why?

7. **Just** and **but** are suggested as possibilities for gap 32. Why is the first word better than the second?

Comprehension Exercise

1. Where does the woman who wrote the letter normally live?

2. Why have her grandchildren never been to the circus?

3. Why did the elephant sit on the little red car?

4. Why was the manager of the circus so upset?

5. What did the police officer think when he saw the damaged car?

Composition Exercise

Write an introductory or topic sentence for a paragraph about what happened when the elephant escaped. Use the answers to the comprehension questions in the previous exercise to help you to complete the paragraph. Feel free to leave out any sentence that doesn't seem to fit in your paragraph. You may need to add some sentences of your own. You may have to rearrange the sentences and find ways to connect them. If you have access to a computer and a word-processing program, you will find it easier to complete this exercise.

Vocabulary Review Exercise

Complete the following sentences with one of the words from the vocabulary list at the beginning of the unit. You may have to change the form of the word.

1. The _____ happened when they were going home from the zoo.

2. We were _____ to hear the news of the earthquake.

3. Every _____ of the family was at the wedding.

4. In spite of repeated _____ for help, nobody came.

5. You should _____ to your grandfather for being rude to him.

6. We _____ them that there was no danger in traveling by plane.

7. "Did you answer the letter?" "_____!"

8. The police officer didn't understand the _____ of how the accident had happened.

9. The judge _____ that the prisoner was guilty before she heard the evidence.

10. Gang members are often _____ in crime.

11. When a child is very ill, a parent is naturally _____.

Topics for Discussion or Writing

1. Write a letter to a friend describing something amusing that happened to you.

2. Tell the story of what happened at the circus with the elephant from the point of view of the circus manager.

3. How do you feel about what happens to animals at a circus or in a zoo?

4. If you are not grown up yet, what are you going to be when you do grow up? If you are grown up, what did you want to be? Did you achieve your goals?

Crime Does Not Pay

UNIT 8

Crime Doesn't Pay

Before you begin trying to find a good word to fill in the gaps in this cloze passage, think about the following questions: What happens to stolen cars in your country? Do you know anyone whose car was stolen? What happened? Why do you think that some people become criminals? You might like to discuss these questions with your teacher and the whole class or with one or two classmates. You could also write the answer to these questions in a journal. This passage is a newspaper article. Pay attention to the kind of language used in this kind of writing.

Dictionary Exercise

The passage, **Crime Doesn't Pay**, is a newspaper article about a car thief showing a group of U.S. Senators how he used to steal cars. Some of the words in the passage may be difficult for you because they have more than one meaning. Read through a list of these words with their dictionary definitions. Try to predict which definition is most correct in an article about stealing cars.

   a. to **blame** [VERB] *North American* /bleim/ *British* /bleɪm/
      i.   hold a person responsible for something bad
      ii. to put the responsibility on

   b. **business** [NOUN] /'bɪznɪs/
      i.   buying and selling
      ii. for the purpose of doing business
      iii. commercial or industrial enterprise
      iv. task, duty, concern
      v.   affair, matter

   c. to **chop** [VERB] *North American* /tʃap/ *British* /tʃɒp/
      i.   cut into pieces with an axe
      ii. to cut into small bits (meat)

d. **conviction** [NOUN] *North American* /kən'vɪkʃən/ *British* /kən'vɪkʃn/
  i. the convicting of a person for a crime
  ii. instance of this
  iii. the act of convincing
  iv. firm or assured belief

e. **demonstration** [NOUN] *North American* /'demən'streɪʃən/ *British* /demən'streɪʃn/
  i. demonstrating (of affection)
  ii. public gathering or meeting to display feeling for a cause
  ii. to show by providing proof

f. **legitimate** [ADJECTIVE] *North American* /lɪ'dʒɪtəmɪt/ *British* /lɪ'dʒɪtɪmət/
  i. lawful, regular
  ii. reasonable, that can be justified
  iii. born of persons legally married to one another

g. **practice** [NOUN] /'præktɪs/
  i. actual use or performance; the doing of something
  ii. something done regularly or as a custom
  iii. systematic repeated exercise for the purpose of gaining a skill

h. **to remove** [VERB] *North American* /rɪ'muv/ *British* /rɪ'muːv/
  i. take off or away
  ii. get rid of
  iii. dismiss from office

i. to **serve** [VERB] *North American* /sərv/ *British* /sɛːv/
  i. to be a servant to, work for
  ii. perform duties (for)
  iii. attend to, supply, place on a table for a meal
  iv. be satisfactory for a need or purpose
  v. act towards, treat
  vi. pass the usual or normal number of years
  vii. undergo a period of imprisonment
  viii. deliver (a summons)
  ix. put the ball into play in tennis or similar game

j. a **tool** [NOUN] *North American* /tul/ *British* /tuːl/
  i. instrument held in the hand(s) and used by workers
  ii. person used by another for dishonest purposes

After you have completed the cloze passage, go back to these words. Did you predict the correct definition? You might like to compare your choice with other students in your class. If you don't agree, check with you teacher. You will have another exercise in this unit in which you will be asked to use these words.

Crime Doesn't Pay

A criminal wearing a mask gave a demonstration in Washington recently. He showed a group of U.S. Senators how to steal a car. The man, who was introduced as Tom Brown, is serving a five-year prison sentence for car theft. This is what he told the Senators:

"I have been stealing cars for many years. In fact, I've **1**_____ over 700 American-made cars. At the time of my conviction I **2**_____ steal any American-made car in less **3**_____ 90 seconds, and I could steal most in 45 to 50 seconds.

"**4**_____ a bit more difficult to steal **5**_____ cars. I have stolen Porsches, Volkswagens, and two Mercedes-Benz cars. The **6**_____ it took for **7**_____ foreign car was about three minutes.

"**8**_____ you know that over a million cars **9**_____ stolen in the US last year? People used to blame the **10**_____ on teenagers **11**_____ took the cars for a joy-ride. As a matter of **12**_____, most of the cars are stolen by professionals. Yes, **13**_____ has become a four billion dollar-a-year business. The **14**_____ aren't sold as such. Within hours after the theft, the car **15**_____ gone. It's chopped into parts **16**_____ are sent to repair shops all over the **17**_____. We remove the identification numbers from the parts and they are sold to legitimate garages

18_____ cut-rate prices.

     "For thieves it's a very 19_____ business. I've made hundreds of

thousands of dollars a 20_____. Now I'm going to show you how to steal

a car. 21_____ at my tools – they're all home-made. Now

22_____ may take a little longer then usual. You see, 23_____

been in prison for a 24_____ and I'm a bit out 25_____ practice."

Language Exercise

1. The words *would* and *could* are possibilities to be considered for gap 2. Which do you think is better?

2. Gap 3 can only be filled with one word. Is it *then* or *than?*

3. Gap 5 can be filled by *American, German, foreign,* and *Japanese.* Which do you think is best, and why?

4. Consider the words *is, was, has,* and *had* for gap 15. Which do you prefer? Explain why.

5. What clues in the text show that the words *risky, simple, lucrative,* and *good* are possible to fill gap 19? Which word is best?

Comprehension Exercise

1. Is Tom Brown the man's real name? Explain.

2. Why is stealing cars such a good business?

3. Why is it easier for car thieves here to steal American-made cars?

4. What is the reason that it may take Tom Brown longer than usual to unlock a car?

5. Where does he get his tools from?

Composition Exercise

Write an introductory or topic sentence for a paragraph about how Tom Brown steals cars. Use the answers to the comprehension questions in the previous exercise to help you to complete the paragraph. Feel free to leave out any sentence that doesn't seem to fit in your paragraph. You may need to add some sentences of your own. You may have to rearrange the sentences and find ways to connect them. If you have access to a computer and a word-processing program, you will find it easier to complete this exercise.

Vocabulary Review Exercise

Complete the following sentences with one of the words from the vocabulary list at the beginning of the unit. You may have to change the form of the word.

1. We are going to _____ that tree down today.

2. Juan Carlos is the _____ king of Spain.

3. The bank robber has already _____ five years in prison.

4. She _____ the teacher for her failure. But she was lazy.

5. Bad workers usually blame their _____.

6. What should I use to _____ the ink stain from my shirt?

7. It takes many years of _____ to become a good tennis player.

8. The _____ of our friend to ten years in prison was a shock.

9. My mother is the manager of her own _____.

10. I saw a _____ of a new microwave machine for drying clothes. It's amazing.

Topics for Discussion or Writing

1. Do you think that criminals are born or made? Why?

2. What can be done to prevent such crimes as stealing cars, shop-lifting, and vandalism?

3. Apart from a prison sentence or a fine, how can criminals be punished?

4. After studying the passage, do you know how to steal a car in 50 seconds?

5. Do you believe that criminals can be rehabilitated or saved from a life of crime? Explain why.

Books Can Change Your Life

The Books that Changed My Life

Before you begin trying to find a good word to fill in the gaps in this cloze passage, think about the following questions: When you were growing up, did you read for pleasure? If you did, what kind of books did you read? Did your parents read to you when you were a child? If or when you are a parent, will you read to your children? Do you read for fun now? If so, what kind of books do you read? You might like to discuss these questions with your teacher and the whole class or with one or two classmates. You could also write the answer to these questions in a journal. This unit is an interview with two famous writers, so pay attention to the fact that it is written in "spoken" English.

Dictionary Exercise

The passage, **The Books that Changed My Life** is about the importance of reading. Some of the words in the passage may be difficult for you because they have more than one meaning. Read through a list of these words with their dictionary definitions. Try to predict which definition is most correct in a passage about reading.

a. to **admire** [VERB] *North American* /əd'maiər/ *British* /əd'maɪə(r)/
   i.   look at with pleasure or satisfaction; have a high opinion of
   ii. express admiration of

b. a **conflict** [NOUN] *North American* /'kan‚flɪkt/ *British* /'kɒnflɪkt/
   i.   fight; struggle; quarrel
   ii. opposition; difference

c. **delight** [NOUN] *North American* /di'lait/ *British* /dɪ'laɪt/
   i.   great pleasure; joy
   ii. cause or source of great pleasure

d. an **escape** [NOUN] *North American* /ɪ'skeip/ *British* /ɪs'keɪp/
   i.   escaping; fact of having escaped
   ii. means of escape
   iii. relief or distraction from difficulties or dull routine

e. an **extract** [NOUN] *North American* /ˈekˌstrækt/ *British* /ɪkˈstrækt/
   i.   that which has been extracted
   ii. passage extracted

f. a **fantasy** [NOUN] *North American* /ˈfæntəsi/ *British* /ˈfæntəsi/
   i.   fancy; imagination, especially when extravagant
   ii. wild or strange product of the imagination

g. **fiction** [NOUN] *North American* /ˈfɪkʃən/ *British* /ˈfɪkʃn/
   i.   something invented or imagined
   ii. stories, novels, or romances

h. to **grab** [VERB] /græb/
   i.   take roughly, eagerly, or selfishly
   ii. sudden snatch
   iii. mechanical device for taking up and holding something to be lifted or moved

i. to **imagine** [VERB] /ɪˈmædʒɪn/
   i.   form a picture of in the mind
   ii. think of as probable

j. to **improve** [VERB] *North American* /ɪmˈpruv/ *British* /ɪmˈpruːv/
   i.   make or become better
   ii. to add beauty, usefulness, or value

k. to **inspire** [VERB] *North American* /ɪnˈspaɪər/ *British* /ɪnˈspaɪə(r)/
   i.   put uplifting thoughts, feelings, or aims into practice
   ii. give inspiration
   iii. breathe in air

l. **partly** [ADVERB] *North American* /ˈpartli/ *British* /ˈpaːtlɪ/
   i.   to some extent
   ii. in some way

m. to **prefer** [VERB] *North American* /prɪˈfər/ *British* /prɪˈfeː(r)/
   i.   choose over another or others; like better
   ii. present; put forward

n. to **recommend** [VERB] /rekəˈmend/
   i.   speak favorably of; say that one thinks that something is good
   ii. suggest as wise or suitable; advise

o. to **terrify** [VERB] *North American* /'terəˌfaɪ/ *British* /'terɪfaɪ/
   i.   to fill with fear
   ii. to be very great or extreme

After you have completed the cloze passage, go back to these words. Did you predict the correct definition of the word? You might like to compare your choice with other students in your class. If you don't agree, check your answer with your teacher. You will have another exercise in this unit in which you will be asked to use these words.

The Books that Changed My Life

Robin Brancato and Susan Hinton are two American authors who write for young people. They were interviewed by *Voice*, a magazine for young adults in the USA. Here are two extracts from the interviews:

ROBIN BRANCATO

When I was a teenager, I read a **1**_____! That was partly because we **2**_____ to a new town at the **3**_____ of my freshman year in high school, and I had no old friends around. **4**_____ I turned to books.

I liked all kinds, but then **5**_____ now I preferred realistic fiction **6**_____ fantasy and non-fiction. Steinbeck's *Grapes of Wrath,* Margaret Mitchell's *Gone With* **7**_____ *Wind,* Richard Wright's *Native Son*, and Daphne du Maurier's *Rebecca* were my **8**_____. Today, when I recommend these titles to my students, I usually **9**_____ that they fall for them as hard as I **10**_____. Another type of writing **11**_____ always loved is humor. Styles change, but my favorite, James Thurber, holds up **12**_____. I recall especially *The Secret Life of Walter Mitty* (**13**_____ is a Snoopy type, forever imagining **14**_____ as a hero) and *The Thirteen Clocks,* a fairy tale. For me, the **15**_____ of books is almost as important as the company **16**_____ people. A good book, like a

17_____ companion, should delight you, challenge you to think, and

inspire you to be a better 18_____.

S. E. HINTON

I loved *Gone With the* 19_____, *Lone Cowboy* and *Catcher in the Rye*

20_____ *The Haunting of Hill House,* 21_____ for a different reason.

I loved the epic scope of *Gone With The Wind,* admired Will James' freedom

22_____ a lone cowboy, identified 23_____ Holden Caulfield's

conflicts, and slammed *Hill House* shut right in the middle,

24_____ terrified to go on! Of course, they changed my thinking – by

25_____ me think. They 26_____ my life by improving my

writing. I was already writing as a teenager – in 27_____, I began as a

child. Books 28_____ everything to me as a teenager. 30_____

have been friends and family, escape, travel, romance, and 31_____ times

a lifeline to grab onto. I 32_____ imagine a world without books. I know

I wouldn't be able to live in 33_____.

Language Exercise

1. The original word in gap 4 is *So.* If you could use a phrase to fill the gap, which would you prefer? *As a result; because of this; as a consequence.*

2. a) Gap 6 is filled by a preposition. Which do you prefer *to* or *than?* Why?
    b) Which verb is it linked with?

3. Gap 10 can be filled by one word. Do you prefer *do* or *did?* Why?

4. Which of the following does the word in gap 30 refer to: *friends, books,* or *times?* Why?

5. Gap 33 can be filled by *one* or *it.* Which do you prefer? What does this pronoun refer to?

Comprehension Exercise

1. Both writers mention the names of books they love. Are there any books that both women mention?

2. What do they say is the best way to become a better writer?

3. Which one of these writers is also a teacher?

4. Why did Robin Brancato read so much when she was a teenager?

5. Which author began to write as a child?

Composition Exercise

Write an introductory or topic sentence for a paragraph about how some authors begin to write books. Use the answers to the comprehension questions in the previous exercise to help you to complete the paragraph. Feel free to leave out any sentence that doesn't seem to fit in your paragraph. You may need to add some sentences of your own. You may have to rearrange the sentences and find ways to connect them. If you have access to a computer and a word-processing program, you will find it easier to complete this exercise.

Vocabulary Review Exercise

Complete the following sentences with one of the words from the vocabulary list at the beginning of the unit. You may have to change the form of the word.

1. Visitors to San Francisco usually _____ the Golden Gate bridge.

2. The children were _____ of being alone in the woods.

3. My husband only reads true stories, while I prefer _____.

4. The doctor _____ that he stop smoking and start exercising.

5. Many people struggle with the _____ between duty and pleasure.

6. Which would you _____, black or white?

7. Music and art are my chief _____.

8. The dog _____ the meat and ran away with it.

9. Most readers can _____ the things they read about. They actually see pictures.

10. Nobody has ever _____ from this prison.

11. You were _____ responsible for the accident because you didn't warn her of the danger.

12. The only way to _____ your writing is to read more.

13. Disney film studios often make _____ like *Fantasia*.

14. What _____ you to play so well?

15. Newspapers and magazines often publish _____ from longer works.

Topics for Discussion or Writing

1. Describe a book you read recently that meant a great deal to you. Did it make you want to be one of the characters? Did it inspire you? Did it help you with a problem? Did it tell a good story?

2. Who are your favorite authors?

3. Which do you prefer – fiction or non-fiction? Explain the reasons for your choice.

The Beat Goes On . . .

U
N
I
T

10

Jokes

Before you begin trying to find a good word to fill in the gaps in this cloze passage, think about the following questions: Some students think that English speaking people have a strange sense of humor. What do you think? What do people in your country laugh at? Do you think that people all over the world think the same things are funny? Explain. You might like to discuss these questions with your teacher and the whole class or with one or two classmates. You could also write the answer to these questions in a journal. This unit includes four jokes. The language of jokes is different from other kinds of English such as newspaper articles or interviews.

Dictionary Exercise

The passage, **Jokes,** is about jokes. Some of the words in the passage may be difficult for you because they have more than one meaning. Read through a list of these words with their dictionary definitions. Try to predict which definition is most correct for jokes.

a. **dramatic** [ADJECTIVE] *North American* /drə'mætik/ *British* /drə'mætik/
   i.   of drama
   ii. sudden or exciting
   iii. showing feelings or character in a lively way

b. an **excuse** [NOUN] *North American* /ɪk'skyus/ *British* /ɪk'skju·s/
   i.   reason given (true or invented)
   ii. explanation

c. to **face** [VERB] *North American* /feis/ *British* /feɪs/
   i.   have or turn the face to, or in a certain direction
   ii. meet confidently or defiantly
   iii. recognize the existence of
   iv. present itself to
   v.   cover with a layer of

d. to **gather** [VERB] *North American* /ˈgæðər/ *British* /ˈgæðə(r)/
   i. get, come, or bring together
   ii. pick (flowers)
   iii. obtain gradually; gain little by little
   iv. (in sewing) pull together into small folds

e. **greedy** [ADJECTIVE] *North American* /ˈgridi/ *British* /ˈgriːdi/
   i. filled with greed
   ii. wanting more than is right or normal

f. **mind** [NOUN] *North American* /maind/ *British* /maɪnd/
   i. person's capacity to think, feel, know, and perceive
   ii. intellect; intelligence; ability to reason
   iii. sanity; healthy mental state
   iv. memory; remembrance

g. to **pound** [VERB] *North American* /paund/ *British* /paʊnd/
   i. strike or beat heavily and repeatedly
   ii. crush to powder

h. to **practice** [VERB] /ˈpræktɪs/
   i. do something repeatedly or regularly in order to acquire or improve a skill
   ii. make a habit of doing what one advises others to do
   iii. work at or engage in

i. **relative** [NOUN] /ˈrelətɪv/
   i. relative word especially a pronoun
   ii. person to whom one is related by blood or marriage

j. **sound** [ADJECTIVE] *North American* /saund/ *British* /saʊnd/
   i. healthy; in good condition
   ii. dependable; based on logic and facts
   iii. capable, careful
   iv. thorough; deep

k. **terrible** [ADJECTIVE] *North American* /ˈterəbəl/ *British* /ˈterəbl/
   i. causing great fear or horror
   ii. causing great discomfort; extreme
   iii. extremely bad

After you have completed the cloze passage, go back to these words. Did you predict the correct definition of the word? You might like to compare your choice with other students in your class. If you don't agree, check your answer with your teacher. You will have another exercise in this unit in which you will be asked to use these words.

Jokes

YOU CAN'T TAKE IT WITH YOU

The greedy relatives were gathered to listen to the reading of the will.

When everyone was seated, the lawyer spoke.

"You'll be out of here in no **1**_____," she said. "The will is only one

sentence long. **2**_____ says, 'Being of sound mind and body, I

3_____ every penny I had.'"

WHAT PROBLEM?

PATIENT: Doctor, I **4**_____ this terrible problem with my memory. I can't

seem to **5**_____ anything?

DOCTOR: How **6**_____ has this been going on?

PATIENT: How long has what been **7**_____ on?

DRAMATIC EXCUSE

Steve went out with his friends one night. His **8**_____ wanted him

home by midnight. But he didn't **9**_____ much attention to the time.

First they **10**_____ to a movie. Then they went bowling. **11**_____

they went to a diner for a snack. By the time they were ready to go

12_____, it was 2:00 in the **13**_____. Steve was worried about facing 14_____ parents two hours late. Then he had an idea. He

15_____ them before he left the diner. "Hi, Dad," he said. "This is

16_____. Don't pay the ransom money. 17_____ let me go, and

I'm on my way home."

THE BEAT GOES ON

ANGRY NEIGHBOR: I 18_____ in the apartment below you.

19_____ you hear me pounding on the ceiling in the middle of the

20_____?

FRED: Yes, but don't apologize. I was 21_____ anyway, practicing on my

trumpet.

Language Exercise

1. What does the word in gap 2 refer to?

2. Why must the verb you use to fill gap 3 be in the past tense?

3. Which is preferable to fill gap 11: *Later* or *Then?*

4. Which of the following is correct for gap 13: *morning, afternoon* or *evening?*

5. The word to fill gap 17 is a pronoun. What does it refer to?

Comprehension Exercise

1. Why did the person who died (in the first joke) spend all the money?

2. What was wrong with the person who went to see the doctor?

3. What excuse did Steve use to explain why he was so late?

4. Why did the person (in the fourth joke) have trouble sleeping?

5. Do you notice anything special about the language of jokes?

Composition Exercise

Write an introductory or topic sentence for a paragraph about jokes. Use any ideas you got from the jokes in this unit to help you to complete the paragraph.

Vocabulary Review Exercise

Complete the following sentences with one of the words from the vocabulary list at the beginning of the unit. You may have to change the form of the word.

1. The dog's not hungry. It can't stop eating because it's so _____.

2. We couldn't eat the food as it was so _____.

3. Students who are absent without an _____ will be dropped.

4. The music was so powerful it blew my _____.

5. My grandmother always used to give me _____ advice.

6. Elvis began to sing and a crowd soon _____ around him.

7. There have been _____ changes recently in what was the USSR.

8. Close _____ cannot marry according to the law.

9. Turn around and _____ me. Did you do it?

10. She could feel her heart _____ after winning the race.

11. My teacher told me to _____ the violin every day.

Topics for Discussion or Writing

1. Which joke did you like best? Why?

2. Which joke did you think was not funny at all. Can you explain why?

3. Translate a joke from your first language into English.

4. Write down the best English joke you know.

Cruise Ship Returning to the Port of Miami, USA

Happiness is . . .
a Caribbean Cruise

Before you begin trying to find a good word to fill in the gaps in this cloze passage, think about the following questions: Have you or anyone you know ever been on a cruise? What do you know about this kind of vacation? Do you know where the most popular areas in the world are for a cruise? If you could choose to go on a cruise, where would you go to? You might like to discuss these questions with your teacher and the whole class or with one or two classmates. You could also write the answers to these questions in your journal. This unit is adapted from an advertising brochure and is typical of advertising English.

Dictionary Exercise

The passage, **Happiness is . . . a Caribbean Cruise,** is an advertisement for a cruise. Some of the words in the passage may be difficult for you because they have more than one meaning. Read through a list of these words with their dictionary definitions. Try to predict which definition is most correct in a passage about a cruise.

a. **anticipation** [NOUN] *North American* /æn,tɪsə'peiʃən/ *British* /æntɪsɪ'peɪʃn/
   i. expectation especially of something pleasant
   ii. something done before someone else does it

b. to **check** [VERB] /tʃek/
   i. to examine in order to learn whether something is correct
   ii. to arrive and register at a hotel
   iii. examine to see whether it is what is claimed
   iv. to hold back; cause to go slow or stop
   v. threaten an opponent's king in chess

c. a **cruise** [NOUN] *North American* /kruz/ *British* /kru:z/
   i. to go for a sail looking for pleasure
   ii. the speed at which an automobile or aircraft travels best

d. to **experience** [VERB] *North American* /ɪkˈspɪriəns/ *British* /ɪkˈspɪriəns/
   i.   to gain knowledge or skill by doing and seeing things
   ii. to be affected in some way

e. to **gain** [VERB] *North American* /geɪn/ *British* /geɪn/
   i.   obtain (something wanted or needed)
   ii. to make progress

f. **momentum** [NOUN] *North American* /ˈmouˈmentəm/ *British* /məˈmentəm/
   i.   the product of mass and velocity of a moving body
   ii. force (as) gained by movement; impetus

g. a **pier** [NOUN] *North American* /pɪr/ *British* /pɪə(r)/
   i.   platform of wood, iron, etc. built out from the shore
   ii.   pillar or structure supporting the span of a bridge
   iii. supporting structure between two windows

h. a **port** [NOUN] *North American* /pɔrt/ *British* /pɔːt/
   i.   harbor
   ii.   a town or city with a harbor, where ships load and unload cargo
   iii. refuge
   iv.   left side of a ship or aircraft as one faces forward

After you have completed the cloze passage, go back to these words. Did you predict the correct definition of the word? You might like to compare your choice with other students in your class. If you don't agree, check your answer with your teacher. You will have another exercise in this unit in which you will be asked to use these words.

Happiness is . . . a Caribbean Cruise

It's Saturday afternoon and you are in the cruise capital of the world – Miami – and you thought the day would never come!

1_____ feel the excitement as you enter the new port area and 2_____ the laughter of fellow passengers and begin to experience the happy feeling of the long awaited 3_____.

You're quickly checked 4_____, your dining seating is already arranged, and your luggage on 5_____ way to your cabin. It seems like you just got here and yet you 6_____ already aboard and ready to sail. If your friends 7_____ see you 8_____.

And there you are on deck happily waving 9_____ as your ship slowly leaves the pier and gains momentum toward the Caribbean cruise 10_____ always dreamed of taking.

You look around as the Miami skyline disappears and 11_____ your fellow passengers 12_____ by. They're of all ages, yet they all share the same exciting anticipation of a 13_____ cruise.

14_____ is smiling, both passengers and crew, and before you know it you are 15_____ friends for a lifetime. 16_____ with whom you'll share your vacation, your shipboard life and the pleasure of your time 17_____ in the friendly Caribbean 18_____.

Language Exercise

1. Suggest at least three words that are possible for gap 3.

2. Which of the following words is correct for gap 5: *it's* or *its?* Why?

3. For gap 7 which is better *could* or *can?* Why?

4. Consider the words *goodbye* and *farewell* for gap 9. Which is preferable and why?

5. Find at least three words that can be used to fill gap 12.

6. Which form of the verb should be used in gap 15: *making, made,* or *makes?*

7. Is the word *friends* better than the word *people* to fill gap 16? Why?

8. The present progressive is used quite often in this passage. Why is that?

Comprehension Exercise

1. Which city do most cruise ships leave from?

2. Describe some of the arrangements that are made when the passengers arrive for their cruise.

3. Describe the mood of the passengers as they leave for their cruise.

4. What kind of things do passengers do to spend their time on such vacations?

Composition Exercise

Write an introductory or topic sentence for a paragraph about a cruise. Use the answers to the comprehension questions in the previous exercise to help you to complete the paragraph. Feel free to leave out any sentence that doesn't seem to fit your paragraph. You will need to add some sentences of your own. You may need to rearrange the sentences and find ways to connect them. If you have access to a computer and a word-processing program, you will find it easier to complete this exercise.

Vocabulary Review Exercise

Complete the following sentences with one of the words from the vocabulary list at the beginning of this unit. You may have to change the form of the word.

1. We walked down to the _____ to see the ships.

2. Does a falling body gain _____?

3. At most hotels you can't _____ in until noon.

4. Very often the _____ of a special event, is the best part of it.

5. Many cities are established because they are on the ocean and serve as _____.

6. Before you look for a job, it helps if you have _____ experience in the field.

7. Every year they go for a _____ to explore a different part of the world.

8. I have _____ great pleasure in my study of music and art.

Topics for Discussion or Writing

1. What are some of the advantages and disadvantages of a vacation on a ship?

2. Write a letter to a travel agent making enquiries about a cruise you would like to take.

3. Find some advertisements for vacations. Study them and try to decide if they are true.

4. Imagine that you are taking this cruise. Write a postcard to a friend describing your feelings as the ship left Miami.

5. Describe the most unusual or interesting vacation you ever had.

Leah or Ya-Chun

"My American Name is Leah"
"I am Leah"

Before you begin trying to find a good word to fill in the gaps in these cloze passages, think about the following questions: Do all children learn languages the same way? Explain. How old were you when you started to learn English? Did you learn it as a foreign language (in your own country) or as a second language (in the United States, England, Australia, etc.)? Is there a difference? You might like to discuss these questions with your teacher and the whole class or with one or two classmates. You could also write the answers in your journal. These passages are personal stories. The first story is told by the teacher and then the pupil tells her own story.

Dictionary Exercise

The first passage, **"My American Name is Leah,"** is about a Chinese girl and her experience learning English. The second passage is Leah's own story. Some of the words may be difficult for you because they have more than one meaning. Read through a list of these words with their dictionary definitions. Try to predict which definition is most correct in a passage about a child learning a language.

   a. **bright** [ADJECTIVE] *North American* /braɪt/ *British* /braɪt/
     i.   giving out or reflecting much light; shining
     ii. cheerful and happy; lit up with joy or hope
     iii. glowing; vivid
     iv. clever

   b. **charm** [NOUN] *North American* /tʃɑrm/ *British* /tʃɑːm/
     i.   attractiveness; power to give pleasure
     ii. pleasing quality or feature
     iii. thing believed to have magic power; good or bad

   c. **composed** [ADJECTIVE] *North American* /kəmˈpouz/ *British* /kəmˈpəʊz/
     i.   calm
     ii. having feelings under control

d. **dainty** [ADJECTIVE] *North American* /ˈdeɪnti/ *British* /ˈdeɪntɪ/
   i.   (of persons) pretty, neat and delicate
   ii. particular; difficult to please
   iii. easily injured or broken
   iv. (of food) delicate and delicious

e. **distinct** [ADJECTIVE] /dɪˈstɪŋkt/
   i.   easily heard, seen, understood; clearly marked
   ii. different; separate

f. to **force** [VERB] *North American* /fɔrs/ *British* /fɔːs/
   i.   compel, oblige; use force to (make somebody) get or do something
   ii. break open by using force
   iii. cause plants, etc., to mature earlier than is normal, e.g., by giving them extra warmth

g. to **impress** [VERB] /ɪmˈpres/
   i.   press (one thing on another); make a mark by doing this
   ii. have a strong influence on; fix deeply (on the mind or memory)

h. **minimal** [ADJECTIVE] *North American* /ˈmɪnəməl/ *British* /mɪnɪml/
   i.   smallest in amount or degree
   ii. smallest allowed or reached

i. **petite** [ADJECTIVE] *North American* /pəˈtit/ *British* /pəˈtɪːt/
   i.   trim and slender
   ii. slim of figure (of women)

j. **to reward** [VERB] *North American* /rɪˈwɔrd/ *British* /rɪˈwɔːd/
   i.   something given in return for service or merit
   ii. money which is offered or given in return for the restoration of stolen property, or the capture of a criminal

k. **tranquil** [ADJECTIVE] /ˈtræŋkwɪl/
   i.   calm; quiet
   ii. serene; placid

After you have completed the cloze passage, go back to these words. Did you predict the correct definition of the word? You might like to compare your choice with other students in your class. If you don't agree, check your answer with your teacher. You will have another exercise in this unit in which you will be asked to use these words.

"My American Name is Leah"

Although I have been teaching English for twenty-five years, I had never had the opportunity to teach very young children. Last year I was offered the chance when the Wicomico County Board of Education on the eastern shore of Maryland invited me to be their itinerant ESOL teacher. This means that I went around from school to school teaching all the international students.

I took over from another teacher, Joe, who was **1**_____ the area. Joe took me to the different schools **2**_____ introduced me to the children. Altogether there **3**_____ twelve children from various countries. According to Joe, most of **4**_____ were making good progress in learning English, except **5**_____ an eight-year-old girl called Ya-Chun.

"She's been in this **6**_____ for over a year now and nobody has ever **7**_____ her say a word in English," Joe **8**_____ me. "Her teacher is beginning to **9**_____ that she's retarded."

When we got to Ya-Chun's school, Joe introduced **10**_____ to her group. Ricardo and Roberto were very lively seven-year-old twins **11**_____ Puerto Rico. I did not envy their mother as **12**_____ two of them were completely out of control. They did not learn much **13**_____ from me until I hit on the idea of separating them. Mayada, a seven-year-old Egyptian **14**_____ looked me straight in the eye and said,

"15_____ is your name?" When I told her it was Dr. Whiteson,

16_____ looked surprised. "Are you a man or a 17_____?" she

demanded to know. I guess that where she comes from 18_____ aren't

too many female doctors. The 19_____ member of the group was

Michael, a happy, smiling eleven-year-old 20_____ had suffered

unimaginable experiences on his long journey from Ethiopia. 21_____

mother was in Dallas and he lived with an uncle and aunt. Michael was one of

the 22_____ well-adjusted children I have ever met. 23_____ did

he find the strength to face life with such tranquility 24_____ joy?

When I saw Ya-Chun I wasn't surprised that she 25_____ spoke up

in a group like that. She was a petite, dainty 26_____ girl who looked

younger than eight. She 27_____ lost her two front teeth, but somehow

that added to 28_____ charm. She smiled at me shyly when we were

introduced 29_____ didn't say a 30_____. The other children did

their best to impress me with 31_____ English, but the little Chinese lady

was so composed that she 32_____ have to do or say anything to get

attention.

33_____ first thing I did was to separate Ya-Chun 34_____

the group. Clearly she needed special attention and I taught her 35_____

thirty minutes every other day on her 36_____.

Her mother was a waitress at a local Chinese restaurant. She

37 _____ have realized the importance of dressing her daughter like an

38 _____ girl. Every time I came to **39** _____ her, Ya-Chun was

beautifully dressed in the latest style: a **40** _____ Chinese-American doll.

I would go to her classroom and **41** _____ she saw me, she would collect

her books and pencil box and **42** _____ shyly to the door.

Where **43** _____ patience came from I'll never know. I worked with

her **44** _____ weeks. Progress was minimal. Sometimes she recognized

words and from time to **45** _____ I was rewarded with a whispered

"mommy" or "baby" beautifully pronounced.

One day we **46** _____ playing with a Scrabble® set and Ya-Chun

was making words out of **47** _____ letters. She had already made pear and

peach and **48** _____ looking for p's to make apple. There weren't

49 _____, so she took out a pair of scissors and a piece of paper and made

her own. That was when I decided **50** _____ there was no way that she

was retarded – **51** _____ fact, I thought she was very bright.

Lesson after **52** _____, we played with pictures, words and letters,

and it seemed to be one step forward and three back. **53** _____ I was sure

that Ya-Chun had learned a word, she **54** _____ surprise me by forgetting

it by the next lesson.

55 _____ I thought about the words of our Supervisor of Schools.

She **56**_____ to say: "Children are like flowers in a **57**_____. They

can't be forced. They will **58**_____ when they are ready – and not a day

before." It's spring **59**_____ and the flowers in our garden have

60_____ to bloom. Yesterday I arrived at school in a spring-like mood.

61_____ went to get Ya-Chun from her classroom for her lesson. When

she came out, I took her **62**_____ and said, "Hello, Ya-Chun. How are

you **63**_____?"

She looked up at me and smiled and **64**_____ clearly and distinctly,

"My American name is Leah." The most beautiful flower in my garden

65_____ bloomed.

"I am Leah"

It's easy to think in English. When I'm thinking I never forget those s's. I

think, "she sits" and not what I usually say, "she sit." When will my tongue catch

up with my thoughts? When I think, I can always hear the end of my words. I

hear **1**_____ say "child" not "chai" which is what I hear when I

2_____ out loud. The teacher says that I sound like **3**_____

American girl. So why do the other children laugh **4**_____ me?

They don't laugh at Jerry. Maybe because **5**_____ a boy. Boys are

lucky. They're stronger than girls. When somebody laughs at **6**_____, they hit them. And then the children stop 7_____. Jerry also comes from

China and he even dresses funny. My mommy 8_____ me good clothes.

The other girls like my 9_____ pink jeans and Nike sneakers the same

10_____. Jerry's pants are too long. They look 11_____ his

daddy's pants. Not pants for the fourth grade. 12_____ nobody laughs at

him. I know he's big. 13_____ than the 14_____ kids. I'm small.

I stand at the beginning of the line. The 15_____ girls are bigger than me.

If they laugh 16_____ me again, I won't invite them to my birthday party.

17_____ only invite the children from Sunday School.

    18_____ Sunday School we speak Chinese and nobody

19_____ I speak funny. It is funny – I can read and write English – but I

can't do 20_____ in Chinese. It's my birthday next week. My mom says I

can invite ten 21_____ to the restaurant. I'm glad my mom works

22_____ a restaurant. I'll invite Teresa and Jennifer. But no boys.

23_____ too rough. And Nicole and Andrea. 24_____ many is

that? One, two, three, four. And who 25_____? No, not those new girls.

They 26_____ speak English and they look funny. I look funny too. I lost

my 27_____.

    Teacher asked me if the tooth fairy came. 28_____ does she mean?

I asked my mom but she doesn't 29_____. She asked me what I want for

my birthday. 30_____ want a talking doll. Maybe the doll can help me

31_____ speak English. Andrea has one. 32_____ says, "Mama."

It has blue eyes. I wish I had blue eyes. My eyes **33**_____ funny. The

other children **34**_____ round eyes but my eyes are not round. They're

kinda squinty and straight. Maybe **35**_____ why they laugh at me.

The doll has curly blonde hair just **36**_____ Andrea's. My hair is

black and straight. But Julie's **37**_____ looks just like mine and nobody

laughs at Julie. She'd bop them – but **38**_____ too small. Why aren't

there Chinese dolls? Cassandra has a black **39**_____. It's got black hair

but it's very curly. You can't **40**_____ her hair. I'm going to ask for a

41_____ doll. She can get anything in Baltimore. Why **42**_____

she take me with her? Here she takes me with her. **43**_____ is my

daddy? The other children have got a daddy. **44**_____ not fair. She says

he's dead. She's got **45**_____ picture of a man. I saw it one

46_____ but she won't tell me who it is. I wish I had a daddy – a daddy

47_____ can speak English that can go to school to talk **48**_____

the teacher. My mom can't understand the teacher and the teacher

49_____ understand her. In the restaurant she can understand people.

She always **50**_____ at them.

At Christmas **51**_____ the teachers came to the restaurant. My

mom and Jerry's mom invited **52**_____. They wanted to say thank you to

the teachers. Next **53**_____ I'M GOING TO BE IN THIRD GRADE.

Then I'll be **54**_____ to speak English better. I know I will. They'll see.

I'LL BE BIG THEN.

Language Exercise

"My American Name is Leah"

1. Should you use *living* or *leaving* to fill gap 1. Why?

2. Which prepositions should you use to fill gap 5 and gap 11?

3. Gap 12 needs an article. This is an idiomatic expression.

4. Gap 22 requires an intensifier such as *best* or *most*. Which do you prefer?

5. Gap 37 can be filled by a modal such as *can, may* or *must*. Which one is most suitable?

6. Gap 42 requires a present tense verb. Which one did you choose?

7. Gaps 45 and and 52 require the repetition of a word. Which words?

8. Gap 65 could be filled by *has* or *had*. Which do you prefer and why?

"I am Leah"

1. Gap 1 requires a reflexive pronoun. Which one?

2. Gap 13 is a comparative form of the adjective. What is it?

3. In gap 17 you need to use the future in a contraction. What is it?

4. What do young children normally lose? The answer is the word you need to fill gap 27.

5. Gap 41 needs an adjective. Which is better *Chinese, black,* or *blonde?* Why?

6. For gap 50 which is preferable *laugh, shout,* or *smile?* Explain.

Comprehension Exercise

"My American Name is Leah"

1. What kind of job does the writer have?

2. Which child has problems learning English?

3. Describe Ya-Chun.

4. What does the writer do to help her to learn English?

5. Describe the progress the little girl made learning English.

6. Can you force children to learn? Explain.

7. How does the teacher know that she has finally learned English?

"I am Leah"

1. What specific problems does the little girl have learning English? Give examples.

2. How do the other children in the class treat her?

3. Who will she invite to her birthday party?

4. Who or what is the tooth fairy? Explain.

5. What kind of doll does Ya-Chun want?

6. Does her mother have a boyfriend? Explain.

7. What does she say she needs a daddy for?

8. Why is she looking forward to being in the third grade?

Composition Exercise

Write an introductory or topic sentence for a paragraph either about **My American name is Leah** or **I am Leah.** Use the answers to the comprehension questions in the previous exercise to help you to complete the paragraph. Feel free to leave out any sentence that doesn't seem to fit your paragraph. You will need to add some sentences of your own. You may need to rearrange the sentences and find ways to connect them. If you have access to a computer and a word-processing program, you will find it easier to complete this exercise.

Vocabulary Review Exercise

Complete the following sentences with one of the words from the vocabulary list at the beginning of the unit. You may have to change the form of the word.

1. If you work really hard, an A will be your _____.

2. He speaks so clearly and _____ I have no problem understanding his accent.

3. A _____ child learns easily and quickly.

4. Her _____ manners made her very popular with her teachers.

5. If you want to _____ me, listen carefully and always do your homework.

6. Although she tried very hard, her progress was _____ and she failed the class.

7. Try to _____ your thoughts so that you will be calm during the exam.

8. When I went shopping in Hong Kong, most of the dresses were _____ sizes.

9. Every year, I buy extra flower bulbs like daffodils and grow them inside to _____ them to bloom early.

10. I think my granddaughter will be a good ballet dancer as she's so _____.

11. Why do some doctors give their nervous patients so many _____?

Topics for Discussion or Writing

1. What is the best age to learn a new language? Is it ever too late? Explain.

2. What is the best way to learn a new language?

3. Why do you think it took so long for Leah to learn to speak English?

4. What advice would you give to newcomers to your country about learning the language if they don't know it?

5. Is it easier to learn to read and write, or to listen and speak? Is it the same for all people? Explain.

Cooperative Learning

An Experience at the University

Before you begin trying to find a good word to fill in the gaps in this cloze passage, think about the following questions: Do all your teachers teach the same way? Can you explain this? Do you welcome new ideas in the classroom? Who are more conservative – teachers or students? You might like to discuss these questions with your teacher and the whole class or with one or two classmates. You could also write the answers in your journal. This passage is a good example of a personal essay.

Dictionary Exercise

The passage, **An Experience at the University,** describes what happened to the narrator when a new professor came to her university. Some of the words in the passage may be difficult for you because they have more than one meaning. Read through a list of these words with their dictionary definitions. Try to predict which definition is most correct in a passage about the experiences of a university student.

a. **anxious** [ADJECTIVE] /ˈæŋkʃəs/
   i.   feeling anxiety; troubled
   ii. causing anxiety
   iii. strongly wishing

b. **authority** [NOUN] *North American /ə'θɔrəti/ British /ɔː'θɒrətɪ/*
   i.   power or right to give orders and make others obey
   ii. person or group of persons having authority
   iii. a person with special knowledge; expert

c. to **dictate** [VERB] *North American /ˈdɪkˌteɪt/ British /dɪk'teɪt/*
   i.   say or read aloud (words to be written down by others)
   ii. state with the force of authority
   iii. give orders

d. **dreary** [ADJECTIVE] *North American* /ˈdrɪri/ *British* /ˈdrɪərɪ/
   i.   dull, gloomy
   ii. causing depression

e. to **flatter** [VERB] *North American* /ˈflætər/ *British* /ˈflætə(r)/
   i.   praise too much, or insincerely
   ii. give a feeling of pleasure to
   iii. show people as better looking than they really are

f. **industrious** [ADJECTIVE] *North American* /ɪnˈdəstriəs/ *British* /ɪnˈdʌstrɪəs/
   i.   hardworking
   ii. diligent

g. **mechanical** [ADJECTIVE] *North American* /mɪˈkænɪkəl/ *British* /mɪˈkænɪkl/
   i.   connected with, produced by, machines
   ii. (of persons, their actions) like machines; automatic; as if done without thought or feeling

h. **modify** [VERB] *North American* /ˈmɑdəˌfaɪ/ *British* /ˈmɑdɪfaɪ/
   i.   make changes in; make different
   ii. make less severe, extreme
   iii. qualify or limit the meaning of a word

i. **mutiny** [NOUN] *North American* /ˈmyutəni/ *British* /ˈmjuːtɪnɪ/
   i.   open rebellion against lawful authority
   ii. to revolt in this way

j. to **rebel** [VERB] /rɪˈbel/
   i.   take up arms to fight
   ii. show resistance; protest strongly

k. a **routine** [NOUN] *North American* /ruˈtin/ *British* /ruːtiːn/
   i.   fixed and regular way of doing things
   ii. regular or prescribed procedure

l. a **scheme** [NOUN] *North American* /skim/ *British* /skiːm/
   i.   arrangement; ordered system
   ii. plan or design
   iii. secret and dishonest plan

m. **sullen** [ADJECTIVE] *North American* /ˈsalən/ *British* /ˈsʌlən/
   i.   silent and angry
   ii. dark and gloomy

n. to **threaten** [VERB] *North American* /ˈθretən/ *British* /ˈθretn/
   i.   use threats
   ii. give warning of
   iii. seem likely to occur or come

After you have completed the cloze passage, go back to these words. Did you predict the correct definition of the word? You might like to compare your choice with other students in your class. If you don't agree, check your answer with your teacher. You will have another exercise in this unit in which you will be asked to use these words.

An Experience at the University

Most of our lectures at the university were dreary and boring. The lecturer would enter the room and begin to dictate and the students would write down everything that was said. Only once during the four years I attended classes was any attempt made to break away from the mechanical routine.

I was then in my fourth **1**_____ and had enrolled for a post-graduate **2**_____ in education. The class was intended **3**_____ for those of us who expected **4**_____ earn our living as teachers. Professor F. H. Morrow , **5**_____ was the new Chairman of the Education **6**_____, was going to give his introductory **7**_____. We walked into the room, took **8**_____ our pens and note-books and sat **9**_____ as usual to an hour's industrious **10**_____. Straight away the professor told us to **11**_____ away our note-books and pens. **12**_____ would not be needed. He did **13**_____ intend reading aloud to us at dictation pace. It really was not necessary. **14**_____ material was available in book form. This said, smiling in the friendliest way, he **15**_____ for a moment. The poor man **16**_____ have expected some sign of **17**_____. Instead there was mutiny in the **18**_____. Not noisy mutiny. Just sullen, anxious **19**_____. No notes? What did that mean? **20**_____ then could we memorize for examination

21_____? His next announcement was worse. We 22_____ to

form ourselves into groups, each 23_____ doing a special piece of reading

24_____ research and, later in the term, 25_____ to the general

class. That was 26_____ much. That was taking the ground from

27_____ our feet altogether. That made the 28_____ of possible

questions when examination time 29_____ too dangerously varied and

unpredictable. A 30_____ of us were flattered by the 31_____

professor's expectations and disgusted with the 32_____ of most of the

students who 33_____ afraid when a university class threatened

34_____ become anything more serious than memorizing set pieces of

dictation. For once I 35_____ myself on the side of authority.

   36_____ of course, I had to choose 37_____ occasion when

authority was hopelessly outnumbered. 38_____ rebels won. The

proposed scheme of work was modified to give a much 39_____

proportion of formal lecturing than had 40_____ originally intended. As

far as I 41_____ discover the explanation of this was 42_____ fear.

Economic fear. Most of us 43_____ poor students. We could not afford

44_____ take risks. We wanted the old familiar system that enabled us to

graduate successfully 45_____ the shortest possible time.

Language Exercise

1. Should you use *it* or *they* to fill gap 12? Explain why.

2. *Stopped, paused,* and *waited* are possible to fill gap 15. Which do you prefer and why?

3. Possibilities for gap 17 are *happiness, approval,* and *relief.* Which do you think is best and why?

4. Consider the words *and, or* and *for* for gap 24. Which of these words is appropriate? Give your reasons.

5. Should you use *to, two,* or *too* to fill gap 26? Why?

6. *Possibility, range,* and *list* are ways of filling gap 28. One of them is not suitable. Why?

7. *A lot of us* has been suggested to fill gap 30. Why is this not correct?

8. The words *were* and *became* are possibilities for gap 33. Explain why you think one is more suitable than the other.

Comprehension Exercise

1. How did most of the narrator's professors teach?

2. What do you know about Professor F. H. Morrow?

3. Explain the way he had planned to teach this class.

4. How did the students react to his ideas?

5. What were some of the students so afraid of?

6. What happened in the end? Who won?

Composition Exercise

Write an introductory or topic sentence for a paragraph about the narrator's experience at the university? Use the answers to the comprehension questions in the previous exercise to help you to complete the paragraph. Feel free to leave out any sentence that doesn't seem to fit your paragraph. You will need to add some sentences of your own. You may need to rearrange the sentences and find ways to connect them. If you have access to a computer and a word-processing program, you will find it easier to complete this exercise.

Vocabulary Review Exercise

Complete the following sentences with one of the words from the vocabulary list at the beginning of the unit. You may have to change the form of the word.

1. They devised a _____ to avoid paying taxes; however, they were caught in the end.

2. My students _____ against all the homework I gave them; but I couldn't change my plans.

3. The Nguyens were really _____ about the new baby's health because she was so small.

4. Jim was _____ that the famous writer wanted to meet him.

5. Elly, take your umbrella. It's _____ to rain.

6. The computer and the fax machine have _____ the modern office.

7. My mother finds the _____ of housework really boring.

8. Only the president has the _____ to make those important decisions.

9. When I tell my son to tidy his room, he gives me a _____ look.

10. The boss _____ a letter to her secretary.

11. You really should hire me – I work so _____.

12. Have you seen the movie "_____ *on the Bounty?* It's about a rebellion at sea.

13. Good drivers don't have to think about what they do as they drive _____.

14. It was a dull and _____ day and Joseph felt miserable.

Topics for Discussion or Writing

1. How would you react if you had a similar experience to the narrator's?

2. How do most college and university lecturers teach?

3. What do you think will happen in the typical classroom in the year 2020?

4. How much do students influence the way their education is organized? Do you think they should have more or less influence?

5. Do all students learn the same way? If not, what are some of the differences?

Graduate after Succeeding at Sonoma State University in California, USA

How to Succeed in College

Before you begin trying to find a good word to fill in the gaps in this cloze passage, think about the following questions: If someone asked you how to succeed at school or college, what advice would you give them? Why do you think some students have to work so much harder than others in order to succeed? Do you believe that your I.Q. (intelligence quotient) has anything to do with this issue? Explain. You might like to discuss these questions with your teacher and the whole class or with one or two classmates. You could also write the answers in your journal. This passage is an example of a personal essay.

Dictionary Exercise

The passage, **How to Succeed in College,** is about the writer's experiences at the university. Some of the words in the passage may be difficult for you because they have more than one meaning. Read through a list of these words with their dictionary definitions. Try to predict which definition is most correct in a story of how the writer found out how to succeed in college.

    a. **academic** [ADJECTIVE] /ækəˈdemɪk/
        i.   teaching, studying; of schools, colleges, scholarly, literary or classical (contrasted with technical or scientific)
       ii. too concerned with theory and not practical
      iii. formal, conventional

    b. **brief** [ADJECTIVE] *North American* /brif/ *British* /briːf/
        i.   lasting only for a short time
       ii. in a few words

    c. a **career** [NOUN] *North American* /kəˈrɪr/ *British* /kəˈrɪə(r)/
        i.   course or progress through life
       ii. way of making a living; profession
      iii. quick or violent forward movement

    d. to **identify** [VERB] *North American* /aɪˈdentəˌfaɪ/ *British* /aɪˈdentɪfaɪ/
        i.   say, show or prove, who or what a person or thing is
       ii. treat (something) as identical (with another)

e. a **quotation** [NOUN] *North American* /ˈkwouˈteiʃən/ *British* /kwəuˈteiʃn/
   i.   quoting (words from another, from a book, author, etc.)
   ii. something quoted
   iii. (statement of the) current price of an article
   iv. quotation mark

f. to **require** [VERB] *North American* /rɪˈkwaiər/ *British* /rɪˈkwɑɪə(r)/
   i. need (the usual word): depend on for success
   ii. order; demand; insist on as a right or by authority

g. to **relax** [VERB] /rɪˈlæks/
   i. (cause or allow to) become less tight, stiff, strict or rigid
   ii. take recreation

h. a **seminar** [NOUN] *North American* /ˈseməˌnar/ *British* /ˈsemɪnɑ:(r)/
   i. a group studying a problem and meeting for discussion, often with a tutor or professor
   ii. a course for such a group

i. to **suspect** [VERB] /səˈspekt/
   i.   have an idea or feeling (concerning the possibility or likelihood of something)
   ii. feel doubt about
   iii. have a feeling that a person may be guilty (of)

j. a **task** [NOUN] /tæsk/
   i. piece of work to be done
   ii. any difficult undertaking

After you have completed the cloze passage, go back to these words. Did you predict the correct definition of the word? You might like to compare your choice with other students in your class. If you don't agree, check your answer with your teacher. You will have another exercise in this unit in which you will be asked to use these words.

How to Succeed in College

When my younger daughter started school, I did too. My father believed

that the only reason for a woman to go to college was to find a husband. He

said, "Learn to cook and you'll find a husband easily." He was right as I found a

husband as soon as I knew how to cook. As many other women have found

1_____, having a husband is often 2_____ enough. My husband

couldn't keep a job and I soon realized that I 3_____ have to work to help

4_____ the family. As I did not have a profession it wasn't easy to get a

5_____ that paid well.

6_____ I decided to go to college. My daughter and I started

school at the same 7_____.

To make some money I 8_____ given some private lessons in

English and I found that I was good at 9_____. Reading had always been

my favorite way 10_____ relax so it seemed like a 11_____ idea to

study English Literature and Linguistics and become an English teacher. I

enrolled 12_____ the nearest university and began my studies.

13_____ my surprise and shame, I soon realized that many of my

classmates 14_____ were younger 15_____ me and not even native

speakers of English, were getting higher grades than I 16_____. One of

my professors explained that I had forgotten how to 17_____. Actually he was wrong – I **18**_____ not know how to think! My education up till

then consisted of writing **19**_____ what the teachers said and then telling

the **20**_____ what they had said in order to **21**_____ tests and

examinations. Nobody had ever required me to think and I **22**_____

really know how to do it. It was painful, **23**_____ gradually I began to

learn. **24**_____ grades improved but I **25**_____ got an A especially

in an exam.

In my final year, I was taking a Shakespeare seminar **26**_____ the

head of the department. We were required to **27**_____ three plays for

each exam. We had to **28**_____ able to explain every word and to

29_____ who had said what to **30**_____ and why. The professor

would give us a quotation and we had to identify it and **31**_____ it. All

the students agreed that it **32**_____ a difficult task and nobody really

knew how to **33**_____ for the final.

I borrowed recordings of the plays **34**_____ the library and listened

to them at least three times. **35**_____ I listened I followed the text

36_____ to my great pleasure and surprise, I actually enjoyed

37_____. On the day of the **38**_____ I ignored the professor's

directions to answer briefly and to the point. I **39**_____ everything I

could in the time allowed. **40**_____ fact, I was still writing when the professor told us to put down our 41_____. Usually I was one of the first

to 42_____ so my classmates looked at me in surprise.

A 43_____ days later I got a message that the professor

44_____ to see me in his office. Feeling sure 45_____ I had done

something wrong, I went to see him. 46_____ I walked in he smiled at me

and said: "Where have you been for the last four years? 47_____ always

suspected that you could do it. You got the highest grade in the class – 94%!"

Then he asked 48_____ if I would like to teach in the department – and

that was the beginning of my academic career. Now my advice to

49_____ is this: when you take a test or write an essay, that is your

opportunity to show your teachers how 50_____ you really are. Ignore all

instructions that state that you should answer briefly and to the point. Give us

all you've got!

Language Exercise

1. Gap 1 needs a preposition. What is the word that usually follows *find?*

2. Gap 3 requires a modal such as *might, would* or *should,* etc. Which word is most suitable and why?

3. You need a pronoun to fill gap 9. Which one is it?

4. An adverb would be good to complete gap 25. Which one do you prefer: - *seldom, never, rarely* or *always*? Explain why.

5. Gap 37 could be filled by a reflexive pronoun. Which is it?

6. Should you fill gap 50 with *good* or *well?* Why?

Comprehension Exercise

1. Why did the speaker's father believe that it was a waste of time for girls to go to a university?

2. Why did the speaker decide to go and study at a university?

3. When did she begin her studies?

4. Why did she decide to become an English teacher?

5. Why did she have problems with her results and grades?

6. What instructions did the professors give about how to answer questions in a test?

7. How did the narrator prepare for the Shakespeare exam?

8. What did she do on the day of the exam?

9. How did her professor react to this change in her behavior?

10. What lesson does the narrator want you to learn from this story?

Composition Exercise

Write an introductory or topic sentence for a paragraph about how to succeed at school. Use the answers to the comprehension questions in the previous exercise to help you to complete the paragraph. Feel free to leave out any sentence that doesn't seem to fit your paragraph. You will need to add some sentences of your own. You may need to rearrange the sentences and find ways to connect them. If you have access to a computer and a word-processing program, you will find it easier to complete this exercise.

Vocabulary Review Exercise

Complete the following sentences with one of the words from the vocabulary list at the beginning of the unit. You may have to change the form of the word.

1. Our students are _____ to take three composition courses.

2. My father didn't think I was smart enough to study _____ subjects.

3. It's important to give small children regular _____ like setting the table or feeding the dog.

4. Many people don't recognize that a lot of our favorite sayings are _____ from the Bible.

5. My favorite way of _____ is to take a very hot bubble bath.

6. The insurance company asked me to describe _____ what had happened to cause the accident.

7. The customs inspectors _____ that they weren't telling the truth, so they searched their luggage.

8. We can learn a lot by reading about the _____ of famous people.

9. Students are required to participate in a _____. They are not allowed to just sit and listen.

10. At the police station she was asked to _____ the person who had attacked her.

Topics for Discussion or Writing

1. Write a letter to a younger friend, brother or sister to explain to them the best way to succeed at school.

2. Have you ever had a similar learning experience that changed your life? Explain.

3. Write a dialogue between a parent and a child. The parent is trying to advise the child who is very lazy at home and at school.

4. What are the advantages and disadvantages of being an older student at a university or college?

Hitting What He Can See

Larry Holmes: Heavyweight Champion of the World

Before you begin trying to find a good word to fill in the gaps in this cloze passage, think about the following questions. Some people believe that boxing and wrestling are cruel sports and that they should be banned. What do you think? Have you ever been to a boxing match or watched one in the movies or on TV? How did you feel about the experience? What kind of sport do you prefer to watch? What kind of sport do you take part in? You might like to discuss these questions with your teacher and the whole class or with one or two classmates. You could also write the answers in your journal. This passage is a newspaper article which was originally published in the *London Sunday Times*.

Dictionary Exercise

The passage, **Larry Holmes: Heavyweight Champion of the World,** tells the story of Larry Holmes' life. Some of the words in the passage may be difficult for you because they have more than one meaning. Read through a list of these words with their dictionary definitions. Try to predict which definition is most correct in a passage about the experiences of the heavyweight boxing champion of the world.

a. to **abandon** [VERB] /əˈbændən/
   i.   go away from, not intending to return
   ii. give up; stop
   iii. allow oneself to feel or act because of extreme emotion

b. an **amateur** [NOUN] *North American* /ˈæmə̩tʃər/ *British* /ˈæmətə(r)/
   i.   person who paints pictures, performs music or plays for pleasure, not professionally
   ii. person who plays a game, takes part in sports, without receiving payment
   iii. person who engages in something without enough knowledge or training

c. **candor** [NOUN] *North American* /ˈkændər/ *British* /ˈkændə(r)/
   i.   quality of saying freely what one thinks
   ii. honesty or frankness in expressing oneself

d. **dignity** [NOUN] *North American* /ˈdɪɡnəti/ *British* /ˈdɪɡnəti/
   i.   true worth; the quality that earns or deserves respect
   ii. calm and serious manner or style

e. **distant** [ADJECTIVE] /ˈdɪstənt/
   i.   far away in place or time
   ii. far off in family relationship
   iii. (degree of similarity) not easily seen
   iv. reserved; not warm or friendly

f. to **eliminate** [VERB] *North American* /ɪˈlɪməˌneɪt/ *British* /ɪˈlɪmɪneɪt/
   i.   do away with
   ii. get rid of (because unnecessary or unwanted)

g. **faith** [NOUN] *North American* /feɪθ/ *British* /feɪθ/
   i.   trust; unquestioning confidence
   ii. belief in divine truth without proof
   iii. particular religion; Christian, Jewish, Muslim
   iv. loyalty, faithfulness, especially in keeping promises

h. **familiar** [ADJECTIVE] *North American* /fəˈmɪlyər/ *British* /fəˈmɪlɪə(r)/
   i.   having a good knowledge
   ii. well known
   iii. common; usual; often seen and heard
   iv. close; personal; intimate
   v.   forward; more friendly than is proper

i. a **legend** [NOUN] /ˈledʒənd/
   i.   old story handed down from the past
   ii. literature of such stories
   iii. inscription on a coin or medal

j. to **quit** [VERB] /kwɪt/
   i.   to go away from; leave
   ii. stop

k. **vulnerable** [ADJECTIVE] *North American* /ˈvəlnərəbəl/ *British* /ˈvʌlnərəbl/
   i.   that is capable of being damaged
   ii. not protected against attack

1. **welfare** [NOUN] *North American* /ˈwelˌfær/ *British* /ˈwelfeə(r)/
   i.   condition of having good health, comfortable working and living conditions
   ii. program of U.S. federal and local state financial aid for the unemployed

After you have completed the cloze passage, go back to these words. Did you predict the correct definition of the word? You might like to compare your choice with other students in your class. If you don't agree, check your answer with your teacher. You will have another exercise in this unit in which you will be asked to use these words.

Larry Holmes:
Heavyweight Champion of the World

Larry Holmes, the heavyweight champion of the world, has an identity problem. People in the street call him George (Forman) or Ken (Norton) or even Leon (Spinks). He says that he's fighting for his own identity and for his dignity.

His **1**_____ follows a familiar pattern among American boxers: Southern, black, poor, abandoned **2**_____ his father and raised in the industrial North by his strong, loving **3**_____. The seventh of twelve children, Larry was **4**_____ in Georgia on November 3, 1949, and **5**_____ up in Easton, Pennsylvania. The family was on welfare. Larry **6**_____ shoes, and learned a little street corner poker.

"He always put money **7**_____ in a school savings account. Larry looked after **8**_____" recalls his best friend and distant cousin, Eddie Sutton, **9**_____ now is Larry's driver and assistant. "When **10**_____ came to any sport, from marbles **11**_____ basketball and even drag-car racing he was number one in the valley. He was **12**_____ natural. He even learned to swim **13**_____ himself. I remember, when we were eight or nine, my mother **14**_____ to give him 50 cents a day to teach me to **15**_____ in the Delaware River. Since then, I've always **16**_____ faith in Larry.

As a boy Larry used to take **17**_____ in street fights. At thirteen he quit school and **18**_____ 14 he began sparring with professional fighters

and signing **19**_____, "The next heavyweight champion of the

20_____." He worked hard: car-washing, truck driving, pouring steel in

foundries and **21**_____ dreamed. "He **22**_____ watch Frazier and

Norton on TV and say, 'Give me a couple of years and the chance.

23_____ beat those guys,'" recalls **24**_____. "But not Ali.

Muhammed Ali was his idol, **25**_____ legend."

As an amateur, Holmes lost the big one, the final elimination for the 1972

Olympics. **26**_____ 1973, **27**_____ 23, he turned professional and

soon cut his teeth as a sparring partner to Frazier and Ali. "**28**_____ I

learned from Ali was the left jab **29**_____ the face. 'Stick and move,' he

used to **30**_____ to me. 'Stick and move because the other guy

31_____ hit what he can't see.'"

32_____ is a good mover. He is a stand up fighter **33**_____

he will work on Ali's vulnerable kidneys and hope, deep down, **34**_____

the referee stops the fight **35**_____ he hurts the legend of his lifetime.

"The old man ain't gonna **36**_____ me," he says; and adds with chilling

candor, "The only guy who **37**_____ beat me is myself."

Language Exercise

1. The following could all fill gap 6 satisfactorily: *repaired, made, shined, shone* and *mended.* Which word is most in keeping with the content and the context of the paragraph?

2. Gap 12 needs to be filled with an article. What does the phrase mean?

3. Gaps 8 and 19 are filled with the same word. Does it have the same meaning in each context?

4. The word for gap 22 conveys the meaning "accustomed to," "in the habit of." What is it?

5. *Before, when, after,* and *immediately* are all possibilities for gap 35. But only one of these words can reflect Holmes' attitude toward Ali that the previous two paragraphs have developed. Which word is this, and why?

Comprehension Exercise

1. What do you know about Larry Holmes' childhood?

2. What kind of sportsman was he when he was a boy?

3. When did he start his career as a boxer?

4. What do you know about his education?

5. Did he represent the U.S. at the 1972 Olympics?

6. What did he learn about boxing from Mohammed Ali?

7. What kind of boxer is Larry?

8. How does he feel about Ali?

Composition Exercise

Write an introductory or topic sentence for a paragraph about the life of Larry Holmes. Use the answers to the comprehension questions in the previous exercise to help you to complete the paragraph. Feel free to leave out any sentence that doesn't seem to fit your paragraph. You will need to add some sentences of your own. You may need to rearrange the sentences and find ways to connect them. If you have access to a computer and a word-processing program, you will find it easier to complete this exercise.

Vocabulary Review Exercise

Complete the following sentences with one of the words from the vocabulary list at the beginning of the unit. You may have to change the form of the word.

1. Teenagers are often _____ when they are criticized by schoolmates.

2. Thank you for the compliments. No, I'm not a professional – just an _____.

3. It often takes a long time for new immigrants to become _____ with new customs.

4. Many refugees need help from _____ when they first arrive in the US.

5. The order was given to _____ ship so nobody drowned. They were saved by the Coast Guard.

6. Parents who have _____ in their children are seldom disappointed in them.

7. When the teacher tells you to _____, you must put down your pens.

8. Malcolm X was a _____ in his own time.

9. Young children usually tell the truth. Their _____ is so refreshing.

10. Daniel Day-Lewis is a _____ cousin of mine.

11. The _____ of people depends on character, not on how much money they have.

12. Because of the budget problem, some schools have had to _____ music and art.

Topics for Discussion or Writing

1. What actually happened when Larry Holmes fought Muhammed Ali in 1980? What has happened to him since then?

2. Write a letter to your favorite sportsman/woman. Ask for his/her autograph. Mention when you last saw him/her in action. Ask when he/she will be coming to your area.

3. Describe a fight or a game you saw to the others in your group or to a partner.

People Movers at Disneyland (Photo © The Walt Disney Company)

U N I T 16

Disneyland

Before you begin trying to find a good word to fill in the gaps in this cloze passage, think about the following questions: Have you or anyone you know visited Disneyland or Disney World? What do you know about them? What are the worst problems in cities today? What kind of urban problems actually affect you? You might like to discuss these questions with your teacher and the whole class or with one or two classmates. You could also write the answers in your journal. This text is an interview, so the language used is spoken English.

Dictionary Exercise

The passage, **Disneyland,** is an interview with Ray Bradbury. He discusses American problems and how to solve some of them by copying Walt Disney's ideas for putting together an environment which humanizes people. Some of the words in the passage may be difficult for you because they have more than one meaning. Read through a list of these words with their dictionary definitions. Try to predict which definition is most correct in a passage about Bradbury's ideas for the future.

a. **alternative** [ADJECTIVE] *North American* /ɔl'tərnətɪv/ *British* /ɔːl'tɛːnətɪv/
  i.   (of two things) that may be had or used in place of something else
  ii. choice between two things

b. to **apply** [VERB] *North American* /ə'plaɪ/ *British* /ə'plaɪ/
  i.   ask for
  ii. lay one thing on or in another
  iii. (cause to) have a bearing (on); concern
  iv. give all one's thought or energy or attention to
  v.   make practical use of (research or discovery)

c. a **challenge** [NOUN] *North American* /'tʃæləndʒ/ *British* /'tʃælɪndʒ/
  i.   invitation or call to play a game; run a race; have a fight to see who is better, stronger
  ii. order given by a sentry to stop and explain who one is

d. a **fantasy** [NOUN] *North American* /ˈfəntəsi/ *British* /ˈfəntəsi/
    i.   fancy; imagination especially when extravagant
    ii. wild or strange product of the imagination

e. an **environment** [NOUN] *North American* /ɪnˈvaɪrənmənt/ *British* /ɪnˈvaɪrənmənt/
    i.   surroundings, circumstances
    ii. influences affecting a person, animal or plant

f. **frivolous** [ADJECTIVE] /ˈfrɪvələs/
    i.   not serious or important
    ii. (of persons) not serious

g. **glorious** [ADJECTIVE] *North American* /ˈgloriəs/ *British* /ˈgloːrɪəs/
    i.   splendid, magnificent
    ii. possessing or giving glory
    iii. very enjoyable

h. to **humanize** [VERB] *North American* /ˈ(h)yuməˌnaɪz/ *British* /ˈhjuːmənaɪz/
    i.   to make human
    ii. to become humane

i. **ideal** [ADJECTIVE] *North American* /aiˈdiəl/ *British* /aɪˈdɪəl/
    i.   satisfying one's ideas of what is perfect
    ii. existing only in the imagination; not likely to be achieved

j. **major** [ADJECTIVE] *North American* /ˈmeidʒər/ *British* /ˈmeɪdʒə(r)/
    i.   (contrasted with minor) greater or more important
    ii. greater in number or amount
    iii. (music) of or relating to a major scale

k. a **mob** [NOUN] *North American* /mɑb/ *British* /mɒb/
    i.   disorderly crowd, especially one that has gathered for mischief or attack
    ii. the common people
    iii. gang of criminals

l. **pressing** [ADJECTIVE] /ˈpresɪŋ/
    i.   urgent
    ii. requiring or demanding immediate attention

m. a **principle** [NOUN] *North American* /ˈprɪnsəpəl/ *British* /ˈprɪnsəpl/
    i.   basic truth; fundamental law
    ii. guiding rule for behavior
    iii. scientific fact or law explaining how something works

n. a **scale** [NOUN] *North American* /ˈskeɪəl/ *British* /ˈskeɪl/

    i.   series of marks at regular intervals for the purpose of measuring

   ii. ruler or other tool or instrument marked in this way

  iii. system of units for measuring

  iv. the arrangement in steps or degrees

   v. proportion between the size of something and the map or diagram which represents it

  vi. relative size, extant

 vii. (music) series of tones arranged in order of pitch

After you have completed the cloze passage, go back to these words. Did you predict the correct definition of the word? You might like to compare your choice with other students in your class. If you don't agree, check your answer with your teacher. You will have another exercise in this unit in which you will be asked to use these words.

Disneyland

This is an extract from an interview with Ray Bradbury, the science fiction writer, who was talking about life in America in the future.

QUESTION: What do you 1_____ as the country's most pressing problems in the next decade?

ANSWER: The rebuilding of America. 2_____ runs for President next time 3_____ say, 'Okay, we've got a war on our hands, now 4_____ go and borrow 40 billion dollars from our weapons for one year, 5_____ let's rebuild every major town in the country so that 6_____ will have a nice 7_____ to live.' That's the exciting challenge. It could be great fun, it 8_____ really be glorious spending the next 20 or 30 9_____ rebuilding the whole country, 10_____ that we will all be madly in love with America again. Disneyland and Disney World 11_____ teach us how to rebuild parts of our major cities.

QUESTION: Disneyland?

ANSWER: 12_____ set an 13_____ for all of us because he cared about the future. He 14_____ two ideal communities which serve as examples of ways 15_____ turning mobs into crowds. Disneyland isn't a fantasy land, **16**_____ a way of architecturally putting together an environment that humanizes us.

QUESTION: For example?

ANSWER: Disney **17**_____ us seven or **18**_____ alternative ways of travelling in the city: the monorail, the people mover, **19**_____ kinds of trams, trains and escalators, moving sidewalks, small motor cars **20**_____ run on fixed courses. Okay, these are toys, **21**_____ nevertheless, the principle could be applied on a larger scale. **22**_____ mustn't look at Disneyland as a frivolous exercise . . . this **23**_____ really cared about us and **24**_____ future.

Language Exercise

1. The word that fills gap 2 is a pronoun. What is it?

2. The word that fills gap 4 is a contraction of two words. What are the two words?

3. Which word is better for gap 7 *country* or *place?* Why?

4. Suggest at least three alternatives to fill gap 11.

5. Could the word *six* be used to fill gap 18. If not, why not?

6. Which phrase in the last sentence tells you how to fill gap 24?

Comprehension Exercise

1. What do you know about Ray Bradbury?

2. What does he consider to be the country's most pressing problems?

3. Why does he want to rebuild America?

4. What can we learn from Disneyland and Disney World?

5. What did the late Walt Disney care about?

Composition Exercise

Write an introductory or topic sentence for a paragraph about Disneyland. Use the answers to the comprehension questions in the previous exercise to help you to complete the paragraph. Feel free to leave out any sentence that doesn't seem to fit your paragraph. You will need to add some sentences of your own. You may need to rearrange the sentences and find ways to connect them. If you have access to a computer and a word-processing program, you will find it easier to complete this exercise.

Vocabulary Review Exercise

Complete the following sentences with one of the words from the vocabulary list at the beginning of the unit. You may have to change the form of the word.

1. What the boss just said doesn't _____ to you, so you can relax.

2. Buying a house is a _____ expense. Some people can't afford it.

3. People who have _____ don't lie, cheat or steal.

4. I'm still looking for a husband. So far I haven't found my _____ man.

5. You could work hard and succeed; _____ you could be lazy and fail.

6. Well, ladies and gentlemen, if there are no more _____ problems, the meeting is dismissed.

7. There was a _____ of teenagers around the pop star.

8. Doctors should not treat their patients as numbers. We want to be _____.

9. Tony _____ his enemy to a fight.

10. They are preparing to help starving people in Somalia on a larger _____ than before.

11. That's a _____ idea – nobody would ever take it seriously.

12. Did you see the _____ sunset? I wish I could paint it.

13. Psychologists always consider the home _____ when they treat a person with problems.

14. Ballets and operas often include scenes of _____. Walt Disney was a master of the art in movies.

Topics for Discussion or Writing

1. How do people move around in Disneyland?

2. How many different ways of travelling are there in your country?

3. What do you consider will be the major problems in your country in the next century?

4. What can we learn from Disneyland to be a model for the city of the future?

Your Daily Horoscope

Before you begin trying to find a good word to fill in the gaps in this cloze passage, think about the following questions: Do you read your horoscope regularly? What do you think of the value of this kind of exercise? You might like to discuss these questions with your teacher and the whole class or with one or two classmates. You could also write the answers in your journal. This text is written in a very different style which is typical of the language used for fortune telling, i.e., it is very vague. No promises are made, but many possibilities are suggested.

Dictionary Exercise

The passage, **Your Daily Horoscope,** is about predicting the future. Some of the words in the passage may be difficult for you because they have more than one meaning. Read through a list of these words with their dictionary definitions. Which definition is most correct in a passage about predictions for the future? After you have completed the cloze passage, go back to these words. Did you predict the correct definition of the word? You might like to compare your choice with other students in your class. If you don't agree, check your answer with your teacher. You will have another exercise in this unit in which you will be asked to use these words.

a. to **adjust** [VERB] *North American* /əˈsdʒəst/ *British* /əˈdʒʌst/
   i.   to change so as to fit
   ii. to regulate (a watch)
   iii. to settle rightly
   iv. to decide the amount to be paid in settling (an insurance claim)

b. a **budget** [NOUN] *North American* /ˈbədʒɪt/ *British* /ˈbʌdʒɪt/
   i. stock of items
   ii. estimate of probable future income and expenses

c. to **commit** [VERB] /kəˈmɪt/
   i. perform (a crime)
   ii. give up; hand over to; for guarding or treatment

d. to **conserve** [VERB] *North American* /kən'sərv/ *British* /kən'sɛ:v/
   i.   keep from change, loss or destruction
   ii. to prepare jam of two or more fruits

e. **constructive** [ADJECTIVE] *North American* /kən'strəktɪv/ *British* /kən'strʌktɪv/
   i.   construction
   ii. helpful

f. a **contact** [NOUN] *North American* /'kantækt/ *British* /kɒntəkt/
   i.   state of touching or communication
   ii. business or social connection
   iii. connection of electric current

g. **creative** [ADJECTIVE]*North American* /kri'eitɪv/ *British* /kri:eɪtɪv/
   i.   having power to create; of creation
   ii. work requiring intelligence and imagination

h. **eventually** [ADVERB] *North American* /ɪ'ventʃuəli/ *British* /ɪ'ventʃʊəlɪ/
   i.   coming at last as a result
   ii. ultimately; finally

i. **forceful** [ADJECTIVE] *North American* /'fɔrsfəl/ *British* /'fɔ:sfl/
   i.   convincing, believable
   ii. powerful, vigorous, effective

j. to **grumble** [VERB] *North American* /'grəmbəl/ *British* /'grʌmbl/
   i.   complain or protest; say in a bad-tempered way
   ii. make a low growling sound

k. **an instinct** [NOUN] *North American* /'in,stɪŋkt/ *British* /'ɪnstiŋkt/
   i.   natural tendency to behave in a certain way without reasoning or training
   ii. a natural or acquired tendency

l. **objective** [ADJECTIVE] /əb'dʒektɪv/
   i.   existing outside the mind; real
   ii. impartial; not influenced by personal feelings or opinions

m. **optimism** [NOUN] *North American* /'aptə,mɪzəm/ *British* /'ɒptɪmɪzəm/
   i.   belief that this world is the best one possible
   ii. tendency to feel hopeful or cheerful

n. a **panic** [NOUN] /pænɪk/
   i.   sudden, uncontrolled fear
   ii. widespread alarm about financial matters, often causing a fall in prices

o. a **procedure** [NOUN] *North American* /prə'sidʒər/ *British* /prə'si:dʒə(r)/
   i. (regular) order of things
   ii. the act of proceeding in an action

p. **receptive** [ADJECTIVE] /rɪ'septɪv/
   i. quick or ready to receive suggestions
   ii. able to accept new ideas

q. a **routine** [NOUN] *North American* /ru'tin/ *British* /ru:'ti:n/
   i. fixed and regular way of doing things
   ii. regular or prescribed procedure

r. **self-reliance** [NOUN] *North American* /'self-rɪ'laɪəns/ *British* /'self-rɪlaɪəns/
   i. having or showing confidence in one's own powers and judgement
   ii. reliance on one's own ability

s. **status** [NOUN] /'steɪtəs/
   i. person's legal, social or professional position in relation to others
   ii. state, as of affairs
   iii. position, rank

t. a **task** [NOUN] /tæsk/
   i. piece of work to be done
   ii. any difficult undertaking

u. a **transaction** [NOUN] *North American* /træn'zækʃən/ *British* /træn'zækʃn/
   i. transacting business
   ii. piece of business
   iii. records of the proceedings of a group

After you have completed the cloze passage, go back to these words. Did you predict the correct definition of the word? You might like to compare your choice with other students in your class. If you don't agree, check your answer with your teacher. You will have another exercise in this unit in which you will be asked to use these words.

Your Daily Horoscope

Aries (*March 21 – April 19*)

Let others set pace at work. An impossible dream may have to be given up.

What is still to come will be better than anything you've known in the the past.

Find a new way of solving a difficult problem.

Taurus (*April 20 – May 20*)

Someone **1**_____ brings bad news may be misinformed. Refuse to panic.

Eventually, true situation **2**_____ revealed. Find way to show close ties

how much they **3**_____ to you and gain added goodwill. Be more

optimistic **4**_____ the future.

Gemini (*May 21 – June 21*)

Be receptive to suggestions of those who **5**_____ more experience. Social

contacts **6**_____ lead to meaningful business associations. Follow

instincts for affairs of heart. You have excellent ideas **7**_____ should be

put into operation quickly for **8**_____ excellent results.

Cancer (*June 22 – July 22*)

Postpone costly outings, purchases. Put more thought, time **9**_____

work. Contact people who can help you. Find best way to handle tasks

10_____ you have committed **11**_____ to and gain respect of

others.

Leo *(July 22 – August 21)*

Learn to be 12_____ self-reliant and you will save yourself big

disappointments. A romantic partner is the 13_____ person to consult

about career change. Study new ideas and 14_____ the most practical

ones. 15_____ have creative ideas that need expression.

Virgo *(August 22 – September 22)*

Show that you 16_____ pride in your work. Keep promises you have

17_____. A time to put more effort in your work. If content to proceed

slowly today, 18_____ goes well. Refuse to get in arguments with

19_____ who never seems to learn.

Libra *(September 23 – October 22)*

Family members may grumble 20_____ a change in routine, but

eventually they adjust to liking 21_____. Try to cooperate more with

22_____ at work and get better results. Avoid one who is 23_____

time waster.

Scorpio *(October 23 – November 21)*

Start early on business matters so 24_____ have more time for recreation.

Be willing to try new procedures. 25_____ honest with mate, or spouse

about expectations and hopes. Avoid unnecessary spending of 26_____.

Sagittarius (*November 22 – December 21*)

A fine day to study 27_____ environment and to make needed

improvements. Stay within your budget. Steer clear of situations that could

28_____ trouble.

Capricorn (*December 22 – January 19*)

Conserve energy, enthusiasm 29_____ important matters. A newcomer

displays interest in your ideas and company. Be 30_____ objective in

your business dealings and get better results. 31_____ for ways to

improve your business status. Show 32_____ you can be relied upon.

Aquarius (*January 21 – February 19*)

A 33_____ day to finalize business, and financial transactions. Assume a

leadership role and others 34_____ fall in with your plans. You may be

anxious 35_____ gain a personal aim but 36_____ be forceful with

others in trying to do so. Be wise.

Pisces (*February 20 – March 20*)

Go after more of whatever 37_____ is you want, 38_____ be

careful in handling varying activities. Think constructively. Do 39_____

tasks early. Creative urges enjoy favorable influence. Conserve money by letting

others 40_____ their fair share of expenses in social situations.

Language Exercise

1. Which of the following prepositions fits gap 4 best: *for, to,* or *about?*

2. Why is *must* not suitable for gap 6?

3. Who does the pronoun in gap 15 refer to?

4. Which words in the sentence does the pronoun in gap 21 refer to?

5. What clues are there in the paragraph that tell us that the word in gap 36 is negative?

Vocabulary Review Exercise

Complete the following sentences with one of the words from the vocabulary list at the beginning of the unit. You may have to change the form of the word.

1. Birds learn to fly by _____.

2. I have a difficult _____ for you. Do you think you can do it?

3. When a new baby arrives, it takes the other children some time to _____.

4. Medical personnel must follow certain _____ to make sure that their instruments are clean and sterile.

5. That's my _____ opinion. I'm not prejudiced or biased.

6. My wife's always _____ that I don't do enough work in the house.

7. Don't panic! This is just a _____ procedure. Relax!

8. When there are problems with the state _____, there are many cuts in spending.

9. It is wise to consult a lawyer or accountant when you have business _____.

10. Many women complain that it's hard to find a man who is ready to _____ to a relationship.

11. Every cloud has a silver lining. Try to be more _____ about it.

12. When you have a problem with a new appliance, you need to speak _____ with the store where you bought it

13. The legal _____ of women in this country may be equal, but socially and professionally they are not equal yet.

14. If we don't _____ energy, the world will be a worse place.

15. I brought my daughters up to be _____. They can't afford to depend on anyone but themselves.

16. Wise students always welcome _____ comments from their teachers.

17. When my mother died I was so unhappy; but _____ I came to terms with my loss.

18. When the lions escaped from the zoo, there was _____ in the streets.

19. My father always said, "It's not what you know, but who you know that counts the most. You must have the right _____."

20. My new boss is more _____ to suggestions than the old one was.

21. I can teach you to write correctly, but I can't teach you to be _____.

Topics for Discussion or Writing

1. Note that the style used for writing horoscopes is rather like writing a telegram. Rewrite your own horoscope in a more complete style.

2. Who do you think makes up horoscopes? How do they go about making them up?

3. Do you think there is any danger in believing your horoscope? Explain.

4. Write a dialogue between a parent and a child. One of them believes in horoscopes and the other thinks they are nonsense.

Taking Care of Lion Cubs

Don't Blame the Lions

Before you begin trying to find a good word to fill in the gaps in this cloze passage, think about the following questions: Are you interested in animals? What kind of animals do you find the most interesting? What do you think of the idea of having a wild animal like a lion as a pet? Are pets popular in all cultures? You might like to discuss these questions with your teacher and the whole class or with one or two classmates. You could also write the answers in your journal. Both these passages are good examples of newspaper English or journalese.

Dictionary Exercise

The following passages are about Africa, murder, and lions. Some of the words in the passage may be difficult for you because they have more than one meaning. Read through a list of these words with their dictionary definitions. Try to predict which definition is most correct in a passage about murders in Africa.

a. an **account** [NOUN] *North American* /əˈkaunt/ *British* /əˈkaʊnt/
   i.   money paid or received for goods and/or services
   ii. counting or calculation
   iii. do well; act in a way that brings credit
   iv. report; description
   v.   according to what one says oneself

b. to **approach** [VERB] *North American* /əˈproutʃ/ *British* /əˈprəutʃ/
   i.   to come nearer
   ii. go to a person with a request or offer

c. **ashes** [NOUN] /ˈæʃəz/
   i.   powder that is left after something has burned
   ii. burnt remains, for example, of a cremated human body

d. to **consider** [VERB] *North American* /kənˈsidər/ *British* /kənˈsɪdə(r)/
   i.   think about
   ii. take into account; make allowances for
   iii. be of the opinion; regard as

e. a **dispute** [NOUN] *North American* /dɪˈspyut/ *British* /dɪˈspjuːt/
   i.   debate, argument
   ii. quarrel, controversy

f. **foul** [ADJECTIVE] *North American* /faul/ *British* /faul/
   i.   causing disgust; having a bad smell or taste
   ii. dirty, filthy
   iii. wicked, evil
   iv. vulgar, obscene
   v.   stormy, rough weather
   vi. unfair, against the rules

g. **game** [NOUN] *North American* /geɪm/ *British* /geɪm/
   i.   form of play, especially with rules
   ii. apparatus needed for a game
   iii. athletic contests
   iv. single round in some contests, e.g., tennis
   v.   scheme, plan, trick
   vi. animals and birds hunted for sport

h. **help** [NOUN] /help/
   i.   act of helping
   ii. person or thing that helps
   iii. remedy
   iv. person(s) paid to give help

i. **an instrument** [NOUN] *North American* /ˈɪnstrəmənt/ *British* /ˈɪnstrʊmənt/
   i.   implement or apparatus used in performing an action
   ii. apparatus for producing musical sounds, e.g., a piano
   iii. means of doing something, especially a person used by another for his/her own purposes

j. **irony** [NOUN] *North American* /ˈairəni/ *British* /ˈaɪərəni/
   i.   sarcastic or humorous use of words to express the direct opposite of their literal meaning, in order to make one's remarks more forceful
   ii. event or situation which is the opposite of what one would wish or desire

k. a **legend** [NOUN] /ˈledʒənd/
   i.   old story handed down from the past
   ii. literature of such stories
   iii. inscription on a coin or medal

l. **staff** [NOUN] /stæf/
    i.   strong stick
    ii. pole serving as a support
    iii. group of assistants working together under a manager
    iv. a group of senior army officers
    v.   set of five parallel lines used in music

m. to **strike** [VERB] *North American* /straɪk/ *British* /straɪk/
    i.   hit; aim a blow at
    ii. produce a light by striking or scraping
    iii. discover (by mining, drilling, etc.)
    iv. cause to sound
    v.   stop working as a a protest
    vi. impress; have an effect on the mind

n. to **threaten** [VERB] *North American* /ˈθretən/ *British* /ˈθretn/
    i.   use threats
    ii. give warning of
    iii. seem likely to occur or come

o. to **trace** [VERB] *North American* /treɪs/ *British* /treɪs/
    i.   draw, sketch, the outline of
    ii. copy something by drawing on transparent paper
    iii. follow or discover a person by looking at evidence

After you have completed the cloze passage, go back to these words. Did you predict the correct definition of the word? You might like to compare your choice with other students in your class. If you don't agree, check your answer with your teacher. You will have another exercise in this unit in which you will be asked to use these words.

Don't Blame the Lions

Newsweek 1980

The first account of Joy Adamson's death sounded all too neatly ironic: Africa's most famous animal-lover had been killed by a rampaging lion. "That's the way the world wanted to see her go out – at the claws of the thing she loved

1_____," neighbor Roy Wallace said last week. **2**_____ Kenyan police commissioner Ben Gethi suspected foul play, and an autopsy confirmed

3_____ doubts. It appeared that the author of *Born Free* **4**_____ been killed **5**_____ a human – perhaps with a twin-edged African sword.

Wallace, **6**_____ saw Adamson's body the night of her death, was struck by the lack of blood. **7**_____ the autopsy, a police spokesman in Nairobi **8**_____ the fatal puncture wounds on Adamson's arm and rib cage had been **9**_____ by "a sharp instrument." Kenyan **10**_____ settled on bad blood between Adamson and her staff as the likeliest motive

11_____ murder. "She was a talented, artistic **12**_____ with impeccable standards," said a former secretary, Kathy Porter. "**13**_____ was always sacking the help."

Police questioned, and later **14**_____ Adamson's driver, tracker and cook. They began to trace **15**_____ former employees, and they also considered the possibility that the conservationist **16**_____ have been

17_____ by local hunters or poachers, whose livelihood was threatened

by her efforts 18_____ protect Kenya's wildlife. Meanwhile, after a small

funeral, Joy Adamson's ashes 19_____ scattered, as she had wished, over

the rolling plains, 20_____ she and her husband, George, raised

21_____ orphan lion cub Elsa in the 1950's and 22_____ the "born

Free" legend began.

San Jose Mercury News (November 6, 1992)

Lion Raised by *Born Free* Author is Slain After Killing Game Ranger

JOHANNESBURG, South Africa (AP) – One of the two remaining lions raised by

George Adamson of "Born Free" fame was killed after mauling a ranger to death,

wildlife officials said.

The 4-year- old lioness, Furaha, and her two 16-month-old 1_____

were shot last week under orders of the department of wildlife and national

parks in neighboring Botswana.

Furaha 2_____ ordered killed after attacking a game ranger

3_____ he approached the animal and her cubs in the bush

4_____ night, said Gareth Patterson, 5_____ introduced

Adamson's lions to the wild after the conservationist's death 6_____ 1980.

Adamson and his wife, Joy, adopted three 7_____ cubs in 1956

while Adamson was a game warden in Kenya.

Joy Adamson was **8**_____ by a servant in a pay dispute in 1980

9_____ living in Kenya's Shaba **10**_____ reserve. George

Adamson, who retired from the game department in 1963, was killed

11_____ bandits in 1989.

Language Exercise

Part I

1. Who or what does the word in gap 3 refer to?

2. Which pronoun can be used to fill gap 6?

3. *At, after,* or *before* are possibilities for gap 7. Explain why you think each word is appropriate or inappropriate.

4. Who do you think the word in gap 13 refers to?

5. Consider the words *some, other,* and *her* for gap 15. Which are appropriate and why?

6. Which adverb is used to fill gap 20?

Part II

1. Which pronoun can be used to fill gap 5?

2. Why is passive voice used for gaps 2 and 8?

3. Can you find another example of the passive voice in this passage?

Comprehension Exercise

1. Who or what did the police first suspect in the murder of Joy Adamson?

2. Who did the police then suspect?

3. After they questioned and released these people, they began to suspect another group. Who were they?

4. Who did kill Ms. Adamson and why?

Composition Exercise

Write an introductory or topic sentence for a paragraph about the murder of Joy Adamson. Use the answers to the comprehension questions in the previous exercise to help you to complete the paragraph. Feel free to leave out any sentence that doesn't seem to fit your paragraph. You will need to add some sentences of your own. You may need to rearrange the sentences and find ways to connect them. If you have access to a computer and a word-processing program, you will find it easier to complete this exercise.

Vocabulary Review Exercise

Complete the following sentences with one of the words from the vocabulary list at the beginning of the unit. You may have to change the form of the word.

1. You can't do it all by yourself. You'll have to hire _____.

2. The police couldn't _____ any evidence that she had killed her husband.

3. Don't always believe the newspaper _____ of things that happened.

4. During the recent election, there were many _____ between the opposing candidates.

5. A microscope is a scientific _____ with lenses for making very small objects appear larger.

6. If you don't work hard enough, your employer may _____ to sack you.

7. Please _____ my suggestion. I'm usually right.

8. Larger animals such as elephants, lions, and tigers are examples of big _____ which are hunted for sport.

9. As summer _____, the weather got hotter.

10. The principal and _____ in my school work very hard.

11. Winning a lot of money at the age of 95 could be considered rather _____.

12. Some people keep the _____ of a loved one in an urn.

13. If you mix with bad company, you may fall _____ of the law and end up in prison.

14. Hercules was the hero in a famous Greek _____.

15. That tree was _____ by lightning in the storm.

Topics for Discussion or Writing

1. What do you think about books or films about animals such as *Born Free* by Joy Adamson? Ask your teacher to show you this film and then discuss it in class.

2. Different societies have different attitudes towards animals. Describe what happens in the countries you know about.

3. In Africa they have a problem with poachers and hunters who kill animals illegally. Do you know anything about this?

4. Some people are very interested in saving the whales, for example. Others work very hard to prevent scientific experiments using animals. What do you know about these issues? How do you feel about them?

3. Describe your ideal pet. Would you be willing to have a lion as a pet?

English-Speaking Canadian Comedian Howie Mandel

Being Bilingual Makes a World of Difference

Before you begin trying to find a good word to fill in the gaps in this cloze passage, think about the following questions: Are you bilingual? What does this mean? Must you speak both languages equally well? Do you know anyone who is monolingual – only speaks one language? Is this an advantage or a disadvantage? Are people's brains big enough to manage to learn more than one language? Which countries are known to be bilingual? Do you know anyone who speaks more than two languages? How many? Which languages? You might like to discuss these questions and comments with your teacher and the whole class or with one or two classmates. You could also write the answers in your journal. This unit is based on a letter to the editor of a magazine and uses the type of English used to write public letters.

Dictionary Exercise

The following passage is about the advantages of being bilingual. Some of the words in the passage may be difficult for you because they have more than one meaning. Read through a list of these words with their dictionary definitions. Which definition is most correct in a letter to the editor about being bilingual.

a. to **appreciate** [VERB] *North American* /ə'priʃi,eit/ *British* /ə'priːʃieɪt/
   i.   judge rightly the value of; understand and enjoy
   ii. put a high value on
   iii. increase in value (of land)

b. **chauvinism** [NOUN] *North American* /'ʃouvə,nizəm/ *British* /'ʃəʊvɪnɪzəm/
   i.   militant and fanatic patriotism
   ii. unreasoning devotion to one's race, sex, language, etc.

c. a **chill** [NOUN] /tʃɪl/
   i.   unpleasant feeling of coldness
   ii. causing shivers
   iii. something that causes a downhearted feeling
   iv. illness caused by cold and damp

d. to **deny** [VERB] *North American* /dɪ'naɪ/ *British* /dɪ'naɪ/
   i. say that (something) is not true
   ii. disown; refuse to acknowledge
   iii. say 'no' to a request; refuse to give

e. **diverse** [ADJECTIVE] *North American* /daɪ'vərs/ *British* /daɪ'vɛːs/
   i. of different kinds
   ii. varied

f. to **enhance** [VERB] *North American* /ɪn'hæns/ *British* /ɪn'hɑːns/
   i. add to the value of
   ii. to make better or greater

g. to **express** [VERB] /ɪk'spres/
   i. make known; show by words, looks or actions
   ii. send a letter or goods by express
   iii. press or squeeze out juice, oil or milk

h. **holy** [ADJECTIVE] *North American* /'houli/ *British* /'həʊlɪ/
   i. of God; associated with God or with religion
   ii. devoted to religion

i. an **opportunity** [NOUN] *North American* /ˌapər'tunəti/ *British* /ɑpə'tjuːnətɪ/
   i. favorable time or chance; suitable combination of circumstances
   ii. chance for advancement or progress

j. **race** [NOUN] *North American* /reis/ *British* /reɪs/
   i. any subdivisions of mankind sharing certain physical characteristics, as color of skin, color and type of hair or shape of eyes and nose
   ii. group of people having a common culture, history or language
   iii. group of plants or animals within a species, forming a distinct type and capable of breeding with each other

k. **simply** [ADVERB] *North American* /'sɪmpli/ *British* /'sɪmplɪ/
   i. in a simple manner
   ii. completely; absolutely
   iii. nothing more or less than

After you have completed the cloze passage, go back to these words. Did you predict the correct definition of the word? You might like to compare your choice with other students in your class. If you don't agree, check your answer with your teacher. You will have another exercise in this unit in which you will be asked to use these words.

Being Bilingual Makes a World of Difference

Dear Editor,

Reading the article "Canada: A Land Worth Loving" by James Murphy (August) has given me so much pleasure. I'm a francophone and luckily am living in **1**_____ only completely bilingual province, New Brunswick. Growing **2**_____ here has given me the opportunity to be bilingual, and I **3**_____ imagine my life without both **4**_____.

There are **5**_____ many people in the world who are chauvinistic about their own language. **6**_____ can't they accept the possibility that people can be bilingual as well as bicultural? These **7**_____ treat language in the same way they **8**_____ their religion. Language is not holy! **9**_____ simply a means of communication.

Not being bilingual **10**_____ have denied me the opportunity to appreciate all the books I **11**_____ read in both languages, all the chills I have **12**_____ listening to Paul Piché's or Bryan Adam's music, **13**_____ the laughs I have had listening to Yvon Deschamps' or Howie Mandel's monologues, and especially **14**_____ all the friends I have made across Canada. My daughter is three years old **15**_____ already speaks English **16**_____ her new anglophone friends. It's a real joy to hear them learning from each other. **17**_____ this article has reinforced my belief

18_____ diversity in language and race 19_____ only enhance our

lives and that Canada has the opportunity to show the world how

20_____ people can live together in peace and respect. In a way, doing so

is trying to make a little heaven 21_____ earth. I thank Mr. Murphy for

the article in 22_____ he expressed his feelings about the most beautiful

country in the 23_____.

Josianne Berther

Newcastle

Language Exercise

1. Gap 2 needs a preposition. Which one usually goes with 'to grow'?

2. Is gap 9 filled with *Its* or *It's?* Why?

3. You need to use the present perfect for gaps 11 and 12. Can you explain why?

4. Should you use the prepositions *to* or *with* to fill gap 16? Is there a difference in meaning?

5. Gap 17 should be a gerund, i.e., it ends with *-ing.* Which word did you choose?

6. Gap 19 needs a modal such as *will, can* or *may.* Which is most suitable?

7. Possibilities for gap 23 include *earth* and *world.* Which is better and why?

Comprehension Exercise

1. Why did Ms. Berther write this letter to the editor?

2. How does she describe the province where she lives?

3. What kind of problems do some people have with the idea of being bilingual?

4. How does the writer explain the purpose of language?

5. How does she feel about her daughter speaking English?

6. What can people learn from Canada according to Ms. Berther?

7. Which is the writer's first language?

8. How does she feel about her country?

Composition Exercise

Write an introductory or topic sentence for a paragraph which will be a summary of the letter to the editor. Use the answers to the comprehension questions in the previous exercise to help you to complete the paragraph. Feel free to leave out any sentence that doesn't seem to fit your paragraph. You will need to add some sentences of your own. You may need to rearrange the sentences and find ways to connect them. If you have access to a computer and a word-processing program, you will find it easier to complete this exercise.

Vocabulary Review Exercise

Complete the following sentences with one of the words from the vocabulary list at the beginning of the unit. You may have to change the form of the word.

1. It's _____ a matter of listening to the teacher and then doing what she says. You're sure to succeed.

2. Age usually _____ the value of stamps, coins, antiques, etc.

3. Thank you. We really _____ your help yesterday.

4. In South Africa _____ relations are controversial and difficult. How will it end?

5. Some feminists call many men _____.

6. Most religious people consider marriage to be a _____ union.

7. We must find an _____ to get to know each other.

8. Some men find it difficult to _____ their feelings.

9. When I think about the first person that I really kissed, I still get _____ up and down my spine.

10. The wild life in Africa is extremely _____. There are animals in Africa that are found nowhere else.

11. They accused her of the crime, but she _____ responsibility for it.

Topics for Discussion or Writing

1. Write a letter to the editor of your local newspaper expressing your opinion of the situation in your area with regard to bilingualism and biculturalism.

2. When parents come from different language backgrounds, how should they bring up their children? Should mother speak one language to the children and father speak his language to the children? Or should they both speak only the main language of the country where they live? Why?

3. What do you know about the language policy in Canada?

4. What is the importance of bilingualism in a world that is becoming smaller and smaller in terms of trade, education and culture?

Do-It-Yourself Home Building in New Zealand

The New Zealand Home

Before you begin trying to find a good word to fill in the gaps in this cloze passage, think about the following questions: What do you know about New Zealand? Do you like to work around your home? What kind of jobs do you prefer to do? This text is written in a very different style which is considered to be humorous. Some people call it 'tongue-in-cheek' humor. The passage was written by Austin Mitchell and this is an extract from a longer work. Mitchell is poking fun at his fellow New Zealanders. Appreciating English humor is considered to be one of the most difficult tasks for ESL students. You might like to discuss these questions and comments with your teacher and the whole class or with one or two classmates. You could also write the answers in your journal.

Dictionary Exercise

The following passage is about homes and gardens. Some of the words in the passage may be difficult for you because they have more than one meaning. Read through a list of these words with their dictionary definitions. Which definition is most correct in a passage about the kinds of things people like to do in and around their homes?

a. to **condense** [VERB] /kən'dens/
   i. (of a liquid) increase in density or strength, to become thicker
   ii. (of a gas or vapor) change to a liquid
   iii. (of light) focus, concentrate
   iv. put into fewer words

b. to **decorate** [VERB] *North American* /'dekə,reit/ *British* /'dekəreit/
   i. put ornaments on; make (more) beautiful by placing ornaments on or in, or by furnishing, painting or papering the rooms (of a building)
   ii. give (a person) an honor or award (e.g., a medal)

c. **to flee** [VERB] *North American* /fli/ *British* /fli:/
   i. run or hurry away (as from danger)
   ii. pass away; vanish

d. a **focus** [NOUN] *North American* /ˈfoukəs/ *British* /ˈfəʊkəs/
   i.   meeting point of rays of light, heat, etc.
   ii. point, distance at which the the sharpest outline is given (to the eye, through a telescope or through the lens of a camera)
   iii. center of interest or activity

e. to **peer** [VERB] *North American* /pɪr/ *British* /pɪə(r)/
   i. to look closely as if unable to see well
   ii. peep

f. to **punctuate** [VERB] *North American* /ˌpəŋktʃuˈeit/ *British* /ˌpʌŋktʃʊeɪt/
   i. put commas, periods, etc., into a piece of writing
   ii. interrupt from time to time

g. a **venue** [NOUN] *North American* /ˈvenyu/ *British* /ˈvenjuː/
   i.   place where an action or a crime occurs
   ii. place where a case is tried
   iii. scene of a large gathering for some event

h. **veritable** [ADJECTIVE] *North American* /ˈverətəbəl/ *British* /ˈverɪtəbl/
   i. rightly named
   ii. true, actual

i. a **version** [NOUN] *North American* /ˈverəʒən/ *British* /ˈveːʃn/
   i. account of an event from the point of view of one person
   ii. (of the Bible) translation

After you have completed the cloze passage, go back to these words. Did you predict the correct definition of the word? You might like to compare your choice with other students in your class. If you don't agree, check your answer with your teacher. You will have another exercise in this unit in which you will be asked to use these words.

The New Zealand Home

The home is the focus of the nation's life. Other countries go out for entertainment – Englishmen to sit in pubs, Ulstermen to murder each other in the streets. Kiwi homes are so much bigger, 1_____ and more beautiful, veritable people's palaces, that the occupants don't want 2_____ leave. The homes are also so expensive that they can't afford 3_____. The home is the venue for 4_____ most popular forms of entertainment: television, gardening, and peering 5_____ of the window. It's 6_____ a hobby you inhabit, and so exhausting that no New Zealander 7_____ calls his house "Mon Repos".

Americans flee the noisy 8_____ to the quiet of suburbia. If you want weekend peace you must 9_____ away from town. The suburbs 10_____ a cacophony of power drills, motor mowers, hammers, carpet and child beating 11_____ revving cars, all punctuated by the screams of amateur roof menders falling 12_____ their deaths. A New Zealand house begins life 13_____ a 1,000-square 14_____ wood or brick box, sitting in a sea of mud and rubble rather like Passchendaele. Within 15_____ the garden is a condensed and improved version 16_____ Versailles, likely to turn Capability Brown green with 17_____. Hand-manicured lawns get more care and attention than the owner's 18_____.

Vegetable gardens carry a crop large **19**_____ to feed the entire Viet Cong

for decades. The house's turn comes next. First a decoration, **20**_____ an

extension and enlargement, then an **21**_____ and enlargement to the

extension and **22**_____. Once the major work is done, maintenance,

redecoration and the addition of **23**_____ occasional bedroom or

ballroom keeps things going until **24**_____ time to move on and begin

over again.

　　　　The **25**_____ home is his castle. It's the New **26**_____

mistress.

Language Exercise

1. There are a number of possibilities for filling gap 3: *it, them, to* or *so*. Give reasons why each one is appropriate or inappropriate.

2. Which is correct to fill gap 14: *foot* or *feet?* Explain.

3. Which of the following words fits gap 15: *days, weeks, months* or *years?* Give reasons for your answer.

4. One or more of the following words are suitable to fill gap 18: *hair, nails, eyebrows, beard,* and *moustache.* Which word do you prefer? Explain why.

5. Answers to gaps 24, 25, and 26 are all contractions with 's. Indicate what the 's is in each of the words.

Comprehension Exercise

1. According to this story, where do people in New Zealand spend most of their time?

2. Why can't they afford to leave their homes?

3. What kinds of entertainment do they enjoy in their homes?

4. What do Americans do to find peace and quiet on the weekend?

5. Why can't New Zealanders do the same thing?

6. Describe a typical garden.

7. What do these people do to their houses?

8. What usually happens when the house and garden are complete?

9. What is the attitude of the writer towards home owners in New Zealand?

Composition Exercise

Write an introductory or topic sentence for a paragraph about the way people in New Zealand treat their homes and gardens. Use the answers to the comprehension questions in the previous exercise to help you to complete the paragraph. Feel free to leave out any sentence that doesn't seem to fit your paragraph. You will need to add some sentences of your own. You may need to rearrange the sentences and find ways to connect them. If you have access to a computer and a word-processing program, you will find it easier to complete this exercise.

Vocabulary Review Exercise

Complete the following sentences with one of the words from the vocabulary list at the beginning of the unit. You may have to change the form of the word.

1. If you _____ into dark corners, you'll find things you don't want to know about.

2. The judge heard three different _____ of the incident.

3. At Christmas many people like to _____ their houses with lights.

4. He killed someone so he had to _____ for his life.

5. We know the time of the wedding but we don't know the _____.

6. Just look at these flowers: they're a _____ rainbow.

7. Don't tell me the whole story. Give me the _____ version.

8. The new baby was the _____ of everyone's attention.

9. The senator's speech was _____ by cheers from the crowd.

Topics for Discussion or Writing

1. Do the people in your country feel the same way about their homes and gardens as the New Zealanders do? Explain.

2. Write a newspaper advertisement for a house you want to sell. Study the way this is done in an English newspaper.

3. Draw a plan of your ideal home.

4. What are the pros and cons of do-it-yourself house repairs?

5. Do you consider this passage to be humorous? Give examples to explain your attitude?

APPENDIX

Key to Phonetic Symbols used in the *Oxford Student's Dictionary of American English*, Oxford University Press, New York.

Vowels and Diphthongs

/i/	as in	**see**	/si/
/ɪ/	as in	**sit**	/sɪt/
/e/	as in	**bet**	/bet/
/æ/	as in	**hat**	/hæt/
/a/	as in	**hot**	/hat/
/ɔ/	as in	**talk**	/tɔk/
/ʊ/	as in	**book**	/bʊk/
/u/	as in	**too**	/tu/
/ə/	as in	**above**	/ə'bəv/
/ei/	as in	**face**	/feis/
/ou/	as in	**home**	/houm/
/ai/	as in	**five**	/faiv/
/au/	as in	**out**	/aut/
/ɔ/	as in	**boy**	/bɔi/

Consonants

/p/	as in	**pen**	/pen/
/b/	as in	**bad**	/bæd/
/t/	as in	**ten**	/ten/
/d/	as in	**dog**	/dɔg/
/k/	as in	**cat**	/kæt/
/g/	as in	**got**	/gat/
/f/	as in	**fall**	/fɔl/
/v/	as in	**verse**	/vərs/
/θ/	as in	**thin**	/θɪn/
/ð/	as in	**then**	/ðen/
/s/	as in	**sauce**	/sɔs/
/z/	as in	**zoo**	/zu/
/ʃ/	as in	**she**	/ʃi/
/ʒ/	as in	**azure**	/'æʒər/
/tʃ/	as in	**chin**	/tʃɪn/
/dʒ/	as in	**just**	/dʒəst/
/h/	as in	**how**	/hau/
/m/	as in	**mark**	/mark/
/n/	as in	**none**	/nən/
/ŋ/	as in	**sing**	/sɪŋ/
/l/	as in	**leg**	/leg/
/r/	as in	**roar**	/rɔr/
/y/	as in	**yes**	/yes/
/w/	as in	**wet**	/wet/

Key to Phonetic Symbols used in the *Oxford Advanced Learner's Dictionary of Current English*, Oxford University Press, England.

Vowels and Diphthongs

/i:/	as in	**see**	/si:/
/ɪ/	as in	**sit**	/sɪt/
/e/	as in	**ten**	/ten/
/æ/	as in	**hat**	/hæt/
/ɑ:/	as in	**arm**	/ɑ:m/
/ɒ/	as in	**got**	/gɒt/
/ɔ:/	as in	**saw**	/sɔ:/
/ʊ/	as in	**put**	/pʊt/
/u:/	as in	**too**	/tu:/
/ʌ/	as in	**cup**	/kʌp/
/ɜ:/	as in	**fur**	/fɜ:(r)/
/ə/	as in	**ago**	/ə'gəʊ/
/ei/	as in	**page**	/peidʒ/
/əʊ/	as in	**home**	/həʊm/
/ai/	as in	**five**	/faiv/
/aʊ/	as in	**now**	/naʊ/
/ɔi/	as in	**join**	/dʒɔin/
/iə/	as in	**near**	/niə(r)/
/eə/	as in	**hair**	/heə(r)/
/ʊə/	as in	**pure**	/pjʊə(r)/

Consonants

/p/	as in	**pen**	/pen/
/b/	as in	**bad**	/bæd/
/t/	as in	**tea**	/ti:/
/d/	as in	**did**	/dɪd/
/k/	as in	**cat**	/kæt/
/g/	as in	**got**	/gɒt/
/tʃ/	as in	**chin**	/tʃɪn/
/dʒ/	as in	**June**	/dʒu:n/
/f/	as in	**fall**	/fɔ:l/
/v/	as in	**voice**	/vɔis/
/θ/	as in	**thin**	/θɪn/
/ð/	as in	**then**	/ðen/
/s/	as in	**so**	/səʊ/
/z/	as in	**zoo**	/zu:/
/ʃ/	as in	**she**	/ʃi:/
/ʒ/	as in	**vision**	/'vɪʒn/
/h/	as in	**how**	/haʊ/
/m/	as in	**man**	/mæn/
/n/	as in	**no**	/nəʊ/
/ŋ/	as in	**sing**	/sɪŋ/
/l/	as in	**leg**	/leg/
/r/	as in	**red**	/red/
/j/	as in	**yes**	/jes/
/w/	as in	**wet**	/wet/